Precision Therapy

by the same author

The Magic Of Mind Power

Precision Therapy

A Professional Manual Of Fast And Effective Hypnoanalysis Techniques

Duncan McColl

Crown House Publishing Limited
www.crownhouse.co.uk

First published 1995 by Ashgrove Press, Bath

Published 1998 in the UK by
Crown House Publishing Limited
Crown Buildings
Bancyfelin
Carmarthen
Wales
SA33 5ND
www.crownhouse.co.uk

This edition published 2001

British Library of Cataloguing-in-Publication Data
A catalogue entry for this book is available from the British Library.

ISBN 1899836187

Printed and bound in the UK by
Antony Rowe Ltd.,
Chippenham, Wiltshire

CONTENTS

	page
Foreword	9
Overview	11

THERAPY PROMPT SHEETS

Therapy introduction (PS1)	13
Therapy introduction – rationale	15
Therapy mastersheet (PS2)	18
Uncovering (PS3)	20
Deepening, compounding (PS4)	22
Closing (PS5)	24
Induction (fast) (PS6)	26
Induction (optional) (PS7)	27
Induction (optional) (PS8)	32
Induction (alternative) (PS9)	35
Deepening (short form) (PS10)	36
Deepening (PS11)	37
Link & connect (PS12)	39
Negative responses (PS13)	40
Ideomotor responses/Ego-states (PS14)	43
Deepening . . . confusion technique (PS15)	44
Elman Pinpointing (PS16)	46
Dreamwork (PS17)	47
Testing for behavioural changes (PS18)	48
Birth (PS19)	49
Forgiveness (PS20)	51
Unrelaxed (PS21)	52
Reluctance to discuss or disclose (PS22)	53
Enhanced coping skills (PS23)	54

Induce feeling (PS24)   56
Private therapy (PS25)   57
Deepening (PS26)   59
Four fundamental needs (PS27)   60
Redirecting energy (PS28)   61
Ego-state process (PS29)   63
Attenuating emotions (PS30)   65
Thumb waggle (PS31)   66
Forgiveness (PS32)   67
Initiating process (PS33)   68
Relaxation techniques (PS34)   69
Age regression (PS35)   71
Physical relaxation (PS36)   72
Forest trip – release repressions (PS37)   73
Changing Emotions (PS38)   75
Previous life experiences (PS39)   77
Slow responses (PS40)   79
Talents (PS41)   80
Guilt and shame (PS42)   81
Success (PS43)   82
New skills (PS44)   83
Improve performance (PS45)   84
Phase X relaxation (PS46)   85
The awakening (drop secondary gain) (PS47)   87
Suggestibility (PS48)   88
Phobia release (PS49)   89
Depression (PS50)   90
Habit change (PS51)   91
Reminders (PS52)   92
Critical faculty bypass test (PS53)   99
Seal-breaking (PS54)   100
Pain relief (PS55)   102
Body image (PS56)   103
Getting problems in hand (PS57)   104
Back to the Future (PS58)   106

Previous Life Experiences (2) (PS59)   108

Case Histories   111
   Case Summaries   125
   Case Results   131
   Questiontime   139
   Suggested Responses   145
   Hints on Lüscher Testing   155
   Analytical Tape Scripts   161

Therapy Tapes   175

Quotations   199

Miscellany   205
   Bibliography   233
   Index by Subject   235

FOREWORD

As a board certified psychotherapist with over thirty years' experience, formerly a Professor and Chairman of Health at the University of Wisconsin at LaCrosse, Director of US Navy Drug Rehabilitation Center at N.A.S. and presently Director of the Psychotherapy Center in Jacksonville, Florida, it is my pleasure to introduce 'Precision Therapy'. I am delighted that a man of Duncan McColl's experience has undertaken to develop this material. He provides a rare and refreshingly eclectic approach to effective hypnotherapy and a welcome source of stimulation to all other therapists who have limited themselves to Victorian-age concepts. I foresee that the book will excite both clinically-trained and holistic therapists to reassess their approach to analytical and healing practice. Like the precision technique itself, the presentation is both practical and direct, making for easy reading and assimilation. It will provide the required stimulus to those who have become outdated or rigid in their concepts.

Those who recognise effective therapy as something more than a job and seek to keep pace with the needs of humanity in a world of accelerating change, will find welcome stimulation in this book. It is remarkable that it has taken so long to awaken to the etiology of neuroses, to the initial sensitising influences. That the earliest identifications based on events in childhood were all so logical should have warned analysts that the conditioned intellect was heavily involved in serving up a plausible but faulty solution.

Henry N. Merritt, M.D., Ph.D.
Director, Psychotherapy Center,
Jacksonville, Florida, USA.

OVERVIEW

Precision therapy is a compilation of many well-known and effective techniques augmented by healing processes that have evolved fairly naturally over a period of years in meeting the need to provide a fast and effective healing and life-enhancing service for clients, many of them therapists, doctors and nurses . . . all of them with uncommon or serious problems.

Clients, in brief, who lacked the time, the need and the tolerance for indulging in protracted mindgames. The aim in precision therapy is focused on stimulating the abrupt shift in personal awareness that creates a 'spontaneous remission' and on achieving this aim, preferably, in one session.

The theme can be used to augment and not necessarily to replace any other discipline. It has been successfully conveyed to experienced hypnoanalysts on a highly selective and individual basis and only to professionals who recognise that effective therapy, including precision therapy, must be subject to continuous review and improvement. It is also recognised that this requires, in the therapist, an unusually high degree of self-understanding, flexibility, dedication and integrity.

It is recommended that you study the contents pages. The therapy summary and prompt sheets are intended to meet most of the eventualities that arise in analytical work. The case histories, with one exception, are provided in summary rather than in novelesque style, pinpointing the lessons learned from them. Drama has been included only to the extent that it is considered essential to do so.

Valuable lessons are learned in helping clients, including hypnoanalysts and medical professionals, who have been subjected to one or several of the types of analysis restricted to the Victorian neo-Freudian concepts. The firmly-held concept, for example, that a protective mechanism of mind represses events from consciousness which are too uncomfortable for the infant-mind to bear is only significant to a minor degree. A far more important and obvious aspect is that significant elements can often fully or partially bypass consciousness. As the conscious levels function strictly on a linear basis, they fail to register more than a fraction of what is happening

11

around. A significant compounding event, for example, that occurred just ten years earlier in the life of a fifty-year-old analyst was entirely outside his conscious recall until he verified the circumstances later. The event bypassed his consciousness, not because it was repressed from memory but because it never registered. At the time of the significant traumatic event, he was blind drunk.

A more serious aspect of the shallow Victorian concepts of analysis still shared by many therapists today is the belief that a sensitising event, to be significant, must involve a strong element of shame or guilt 'to be repressed'. In effective healing-therapy, any element of shame or guilt clearly telegraphs a compounding event. The sensitising event will be earlier and it will have induced strong feelings of fear or shock.

The too-common practice of merely revealing a shameful event to the client's consciousness and providing ego-boosting suggestions is as effective as dead-heading weeds in a flower-bed. Shame and guilt are shallow-minded concepts, part of our socio-religious conditioning, part of the charade, and our ego is part of the problem, not part of the healing.

The real sensitising events are seeded deeply. Threat-to-life-influences are invariably involved. If they are not released to consciousness, like the roots of a dead-headed weed, they will develop again.

Precision therapy is designed to deal with the root of the problem.

Care has been taken throughout to avoid the herd-mind trap of attempting to describe or define hypnosis. As conscious or our usual everyday state of unconscious self-hypnosis, like love and other forms of confusion, is a natural state of whatever the human mind is constrained to be, something of the unknown and the unintentional inevitably creeps into it. Unavoidably, the same will have happened to this book.

Duncan McColl

Therapy Introduction

Prompt Sheet 1

1. Do you want to live to be a hundred?

2. Breath cycle – in – out . . . is that right? Hand move . . . left – right . . . correct?

3. Which is your dominant arm – the stronger? Press the palms of your hands together . . . why can't you push the weaker arm away?

4. **Visualising . . . know what a telephone looks like? A tree? A flower?** (*The word conveys*)

5. **'Hold up your hand.'** (*Place yours against it. Client will tend to push . . . to resist*).

6. Stress check/reciprocal relaxation/spread fingers.

7. Diaphragmatic breathing/creative relaxation.

8. Fist closed . . . not a heart . . . hand open . . . not a heart. Close – stop – open – stop – close, that's a heart.

9. Hold up open hand . . . what's the important feature?

10. Go to fingers . . . sense tingling.

11. Frown – smile . . . sense difference.

12. Lock hands . . . lock mind so that hands are locked together.

13. Relax . . . anytime . . . creatively/tuned in . . . not tuned out . . . enhanced conscious awareness . . . next step?

14. Two states at this level . . . conscious or unconscious self-hypnosis.

15. **The hand support . . . arm should drop** (*Holding one with the other to illustrate relaxation*).

16. What will be different when change occurs?

17. To change . . . we initiate a process of change.

THERAPY INTRODUCTION – RATIONALE

The objective here is to illustrate the inherent simplicity of the natural healing and problem-solving processes . . . the simple things we tend to overlook in our search for answers. Only some of the points need to be mentioned. It can be useful to include anyone accompanying the client in the introduction.

1. You are seeking an unqualified response. A common one is: 'Yes . . . but not if I have to be a burden to anyone else.' The point here is that we can (at least) influence our own destiny. One eighty-year-old widow answered: 'Yes, young man . . . but why are you limiting me?'

2. Illustrate by moving your hand left . . . right . . . left. Breathing is a four-cycle process . . . in, stop, out, stop. The hand movement is left . . . stop . . . right . . . stop. Significance? Later.

3. You have developed one arm more than the other . . . but there is only one energy . . . for you to direct as you choose. The same rule applies to your psychic energy, to your mindpower. You have fed the linear brain more than your creative, inspirational brain.

    Your dominant hand . . . left or right? Right. OK. Start consciously favouring your left hand whenever you can . . . give it more to do . . . you'll be surprised how soon you become ambidextrous . . . mentally as well.

4. Particularly with seriously-ill clients, there is a need to dispel immediately the thought that there is any need to create three-or four-dimensional objects in the air, or that there is any value whatsoever in attempting to do so.

5. Point out that you merely asked the client to hold up his hand. You did not ask him to push against yours. We tend to resist. Creative relaxation is a state of 'let-go'.

6. How do you relax your hand? You do something first . . . you spread your fingers apart, then you stop doing it and relaxation happens.

7. You take conscious control of a normally subconscious process . . . for two or three breaths . . . expanding the diaphragm then

allowing it to relax. You override the startle pattern you developed as a child . . . you condition the physical centre of your emotions to relax.

8. At this vibrational level of reality, learn to go with the natural rhythm in whatever you do.

9. The hand, itself, is temporal. The space, the 'nothingness', like the stop in the breathing rhythm, is where it comes from and where it goes.

    (Today a chicken, tomorrow a feather duster . . . a perpetual process of change and renewal).

10. Allow one arm to dangle by your side . . . be aware of the tingling sensation at your fingertips – perhaps a slight pins-and-needles feeling . . . as the blood circulates down there at your fingertips. And as you focus on the tingling sensation, notice that you are hearing me better and I am speaking more clearly as we both move onto the same waveband, because the tingling feeling is the result of you directing part of your thinking process, your psychic energies, to alter the vibrational levels at your fingertips . . . bypassing the thinking-guessing mind and moving more into touch with your senses. And it is your sensing system, not your conditioned thinking mind, that you will learn today to use to see your best options in life.

11. Do it.

12. Clasp your hands together for a moment and at the count of three I'm going to ask you to lock your mind on the thought that your hands are locked tightly together and the harder you try to release them the tighter they get . . . 1 . . . 2 . . . 3 (click fingers) . . . just lock your mind on the thought that your hands are locked tightly together and try to release them and find that they lock together even more . . . tighter and tighter . . . that's right – really try . . . and now relax . . . and allow your hands to unlock. Fine . . . you accepted my suggestion because you wanted to . . . and subcon will ensure that you only accept suggestions from me that are for your health and wellbeing.

    (Or: Good. You pulled your hands apart because you rejected my suggestion . . . that's fine. It highlights the fact that you can't be forced to do anything against your will in hypnosis . . . conscious self-hypnosis is a consent state, it requires relaxation and acceptance. So this time, as I repeat the suggestion, just resolve that you would like it to work for you).

13. Next step – spontaneous right action.

14. The more you capture the knack of conscious self-hypnosis . . . the more you realise that you have been unconsciously self-hypnotised at least since birth.

15. Testing for phase one, physical relaxation . . . both arms must be lazy, limp and relaxed. It may be necessary to illustrate this by holding one of your own arms . . . and allowing it to flop down on your lap.

    (Other processes, later).

16. Sometimes worth enquiring, to see if any focus has been directed positively.

17. Emphasise that you are an analyst. You are neither a counsellor nor an adviser. Your function is to illustrate clearly how the client can initiate a process of change. The choices he makes are strictly part of his own birthright. His own powerhouse mind is always his best guide. You will help him to find this source of truth and trust and inspiration in himself. The objective: to bring a great quality and intensity of experience back to the client's lifestyle.

Therapy Mastersheet

Prompt Sheet 2

- Relax – Phase I . . . II . . . where on 10–0 scale?
  Colour of ruler?

- Visualise? Apple . . . tree . . . mountain.

- Phase III basement
  Working level
      Unsettled . . . concerns?
  Each breath . . . deeper.

- First day at school . . .
  Thumb waggle if discomfort or concern.

- Feeling associated with problem?
  Back to first time the feeling arose . . .
  Count back . . . younger . . .
  Relax and dream . . .
  Sub-basement . . . through the zero . . . back.
  Tap forehead . . . spell out word that links to cause.
  Stiffen finger . . . can't bend when open eyes.
  Place finger under subcon control.
  Yes finger – no finger – question, ego state?

- Rebirth – Heartbeat?
  10–0 where at now?
  Fake count up 0–4 down . . . down . . . down.
  Sleep state.
  Symbol of major problem . . . 1 . . . 2 . . . 3 . . .*
  Back to before problem . . .
  Video scene.
  Reveal to consciousness . . . one year's time?
  Future pace.

- In touch with body . . . toes . . . hands . . . lips . . . etc.

Sunlight to discomfort.
Pineal gland . . . pinpoints of light.
Back to happy time . . . birthday/Christmas . . . age?
Did you know what the problem was then?
Forward to pinpoint event.

- Video . . . what could happen to throw a scare.
  Inside body to area of discomfort – Report, where in body the feeling?
  Talk to the part involved.
  Move 3 months . . . 5 years ahead.
  (No malignancy in nature. 98% of the body is less than 3 months old).

- Repetitive dream? Re-dream it.
  Trace 'A' on hand . . . erase . . . say alphabet (omits 'A'?)
  Trip out of body.
  Link to all events.

- Merge polar opposites.
  Bossman–Cleric–Lawyer–Flagstones.
  Four Lüscher fundamentals.
  Early conditioning . . . 'gameplay' etc.

- All repressions released? Physically?
  What do you want to do to him/her?
  Gestalt clear . . . gestalt childmind.

- Anchor success . . . love . . . ecstasy . . . multiply intensity.
  Express it . . . (not in words).
  Future pace – paint heavy problem – override it.
  Any other problem? . . . questions?
  7 days ahead . . . benefits? Swish pattern needed?
  More deeply relaxed than ever before.
  Do you do better than well? *I excel!!!!* **Convince me.**

RATIONALE

A master prompt sheet is prepared for a specific type of client; in this case, a client with a physical malfunction. With experience, the mastersheet can be further reduced and eventually discarded entirely.

Further optional prompt sheets are provided for use in therapy sessions (PS 3 & 4) followed by a selection of more detailed scripts, the gist of which can soon be committed to memory.

Uncovering

Prompt Sheet 3

- Age regress to an earlier time . . .
  Birthday . . . first walk . . . at home on Sunday . . .
  First day at school (may be unhappy).

- Pinpoint . . . back to before the problem.
  Bracket it between two age dates.
  Find age . . . back to just before.

- Tap forehead . . . spell out word or phrase that is the link to the root cause(s) . . . or representation of cause.
  (Or . . . symbol will spring to mind).
  'Nothing' . . . raise/drop arm . . . 'there you are'.

- AFFECT BRIDGE . . . FINGER SIGNALS . . . EGO STATE

- Visit part . . . go down inside . . . report.

- Reluctance? OK to bring this to consciousness in a year's time (forward a year).

- Sleep and dream.

- Test for amnesia . . . 'write' on palm, telephone number.

- Put into a sleep state.

- Client . . . talk to problem . . . gestalt style: what – on the one hand think . . . other feel.
  (Nod when person/problem is there).

- Tap . . . a representation of the part . . . (when can talk to me say . . . 'I'm here').

- Video scene . . . [anything being blocked from consciousness – your thumbs waggle (blush)].

- NLP . . . pictures . . . spin away neg. Enlarge OK state.

- Anchor.

- Timeline . . . eliminate guilt . . . forward without . . . keyword . . . successful event . . . future pace (test anchor).

- Merge polar opposites . . . imaginary scene.

- Retrigger . . . attenuate it . . . relive several times **(Seek the scare) . . . key word . . . override it.**

Deepening – Compounding

Prompt Sheet 4

'Awareness increases with each breath that you take and you can go to any event in your life'.

Stress check. Relax any area of tension.

Lift/drop arm.

Touch forehead (First letter – quickly now).
Touch hand.

Ruler . . . 10–0 . . . Where at? Colour?

Thumb waggle/face blush if conscious mind interference.

Around body awareness.

30 seconds – relax and dream.

'Wheel breathing'. First day at school.

Try to raise left leg. First time explored Mum/Dad's bedroom.

Sleep . . . get in touch from within/dream.

Back to Sunday at home as a child.

Deep breath . . . focus on outgoing breath.

Bring on – dispel emotion/feelings associated/intensify.

Countdown 8–1–Zero.

Stiffen finger – eyes open – won't bend.

Look into darkness . . . pineal/third eye.

Arm, lock – relax as you lower it.

Balloon tied to arm . . . hand touch cheek.

Fake count-up (1 2 3 4 then 3 2 1 . . . zero DOWN).

Basement level of relaxation/test eyes/leg.

Trace letter 'A' on back of hand – erase (from hand/thoughts. Eyes open . . . what are the first three letters of the alphabet?).

Open eyes . . . blink . . . double relaxation . . . close.

Float up – visit around – space.

What think – versus feel – head/heart talk.

Feel growing smaller . . . younger.

Bring sunlight down and all around.

Child within – float to other side of room. Return and embrace.

Whenever I say relax . . . go seven times deeper.

Sub-basement – other side of zero – return to working level.

Each breath taking you deeper.

Go to a holiday time.

Any fun time you would like to re-experience?

OK to bring to consciousness . . . 12 months . . . with increased understanding?

Future pace 12 months.

Induce sleep state.

Closing

Prompt Sheet 5

1. **Back to ISE . . .** *(Physical influence to release)* **. . . follow through on the linkages . . . ISE/compounding, all parts benefiting.**

   Forgiveness (*not necessarily excuse***) integrate the child within, always in your heart.**

2. **Ask subcon** – *Anything else needs to be clarified?*

   – *Clear through dreams and experiences.*

   – *Notify changes in habits and behavioural patterns.*

   – *Maintaining channel open . . . keyword 'relax'.*

3. **Have you any questions for me . . . or subcon?**

   Thank subcon.

   Future pace to disturbing/similar event . . . test keyword.

   Relax – and you know you will attain to spontaneous right action . . . **now** . . . and in the future.

   More at ease with yourself . . . (etc.). You are freed from self-limiting influences of the past . . . the past is freed from you.

   Relax and forgive . . . live and let live.

4. **Everything useful that you have experienced today is part of your everyday living reality and those experiences that upset or inhibited you in the past now serve to increase your self-confidence and success in life.**

5. **So what are we all – we are all children of stardust – and all the joy and love and hope in the world is yours . . . and now you will be more poised, more serene, more loving and compas-**

sionate than ever before. You do better than well – you excel. When you open your eyes in a moment, you will know that you have established contact with your own control mind and this two-way communication channel will serve you well.

6. With a smile on your face and a song in your heart – come back to this world of everyday living reality at the count of five – rejuvenated – revitalised – renewed – and notice how good you feel . . . and the number is one . . .

7. *Test anchors, future pace. 'I excel' . . . convince me.*

Induction (fast)

Prompt Sheet 6

Now just relax and release all that surface tension as you close your eyes . . . close your eyes now and relax them to the point where they just won't work and when you're sure that they won't work – test them – just try to open them – that's right – really try . . . now stop trying and let that feeling of relaxation pass all the way down to your toes and notice how good you feel just with that simple process of relaxation – taking time out for yourself. Now, draw in a long, slow, deep breath and allow your stomach to relax and expand . . . and slowly exhale and feel your entire bodymind system relax . . . Now . . . in a moment I'll ask you to open your eyes and I'll say 'double your state of relaxation' and **each time I do** you'll close your eyes and go still deeper into relaxation . . . so . . . just open your eyes . . . double your state of relaxation . . . now . . . close your eyes . . . that's good . . . and again . . . open your eyes . . . double your state of relaxation . . . now close your eyes . . . and again . . . open your eyes . . . double your state of relaxation . . . now close your eyes. Now . . . in a moment . . . I'm going to pick up one of your arms and if you're truly relaxed . . . it will be lazy . . . limp and relaxed . . . that's great . . . that's an excellent state of relaxation (or: there's muscle tension there . . . just let that arm go lazy, limp and relaxed . . . **that's better** . . . now notice the difference . . . lazy . . . limp . . . relaxed . . . wonderful) . . . now – as I let your arm drop back on your lap – go ten times deeper into relaxation and notice how good you feel.

And now your other arm – good – excellent – and go ten times deeper as your arm drops back on your lap. **Now, mentally count from one to three with me and feel yourself drifting deeper and deeper . . . 1 . . . 2 . . . 3 . . . deeper . . . still drifting deeper into relaxation.**

Induction (Optional)

Prompt Sheet 7

The objective is to induce physical, mental and emotional relaxation and the Elman technique is particularly useful for achieving these levels fast. With many clients, a simple count-down from eight to one, interspersed with 'drifting deeper and deeper, into a relaxed state of creative relaxation' and similar suggestions, can be equally effective. Elements from the following theme have been found useful in working with intellectually-minded and other clients who find it difficult to relax mentally.

As you hear me talk, I know that your intellectually-conditioned levels of mind are actively engaged in assessing my words . . . and in the same way, you can control that level to the extent that – as I talk to you – you can also count the number of breaths that you take – start doing that now mentally or count the inhalation as 'one', the exhalation as 'two', if you like . . . and keep on counting as I talk. And you know, of course, that your heart is beating . . . focus on counting the heartbeats too . . . and of course you find that you can't . . . AND THAT'S THE LEVEL OF MINDPOWER YOU HAVE BEEN USING TO FIND YOUR WAY THROUGH LIFE . . . YOUR LINEAR-CONDITIONED, INTELLECTUAL MIND-LEVEL. It's linked to your outer senses . . . to your sense of touch, of taste and sight and sound and smell. You have a sensory system – a vast inner sensing system – that makes any miracle you have ever heard about seem trivial. Just for the record : it is a system that controls 50 trillion intelligent cells . . . ten thousand times more cells than the Earth's population . . . each cell capable of five hundred spontaneous functions. One hundred thousand discrete chemical changes take place, under direction, in your body every second. There are fourteen billion possible nerve responses . . . that's fourteen hundred times more communication channels than the world's telephone system . . . and your heart pumps 45 million gallons of blood in 50 years . . . it pumps 35 million times a year and up to 4 million times more if you are stressed. THAT

SENSORY LEVEL IS AVAILABLE FOR YOU TO USE. You are not just an entity that has to learn everything by rote . . . by imitation. You are a storehouse of vast creative intelligence and life-energy, capable of INSIGHT, INTUITION, INSPIRATION . . . and you have a personal key. My function is a simple one. To show you how to use it.

Now this time, as you focus for a moment on your breathing pattern . . . allow your stomach to relax and expand as you inhale . . . and as you exhale, allow the sense of peace and relaxation to spread gently to every nerve and cell and system of the body . . . taking time out – time out for yourself.

Simply by focusing conscious awareness for a moment on your breathing, you convey to all levels of mind that you want to relax . . . creatively . . . and you will accept only those words that ring true with subcon – with your subconscious control mind, with that centre of power, of eternal truth and trust in yourself . . . accepting for implementation only those suggestions that are beneficial and appropriate for ensuring your vibrant good health and for maintaining harmony and balance throughout your entire bodymind system.

Now – at some time in the past, perhaps in the distant past . . . you experienced a deeper sense of creative relaxation than this . . . a natural state . . . perhaps free from the world of words . . . allow subcon to take you there as you gently inhale . . . inhale lifeforce . . . prolonging the outgoing breath . . . drifting deeper now .. for the benefit of the entire bodymind system . . . more at one with everything, with everything in this everyday new miracle of life.

Now – gently raise the corners of your lips in a tiny smile . . . and send a message of peace and pleasure to every cell and system and function of the body – a gentle feeling of bliss. That feeling is healing . . . as you become more deeply aware of your senses, of your internal sensory system – freeing the two-way channel to creative mind . . . to the other side of your reality . . . to the side that is always in touch with source.

The answers we seek are all in the mind . . . but not in those levels of mind to which we have conscious access . . . we must seek deeper than this . . . beyond the barriers of second-hand thoughts and social conditioning. Without insight, all our decisions are based on insufficient data. We can do better than that . . . much better than that.

Now, in a moment, I will reach forward and touch you gently on the forehead in the area of the pineal gland, and the moment I touch your forehead a word will spring to mind that will link and connect to the cause of your major problem – to the initial sensitising event – (tap) . . . What's the word? (you'll know it at the count of three . . . 1 . . . 2 . . . 3 . . . *).

Now watch . . . as I raise and drop your arm . . . you will see the connection . . . there you are . . . what's the connection?

AN ALTERNATIVE

Focus on the word/phrase as I count you down from six to one . . . six to one . . . zero . . . counting 6 . . . and you feel yourself becoming smaller and smaller – younger and younger – arms and legs and body – smaller and younger . . . 5 . . . going back in time to the causal event . . . 4 . . . and the word that links to it is xxxxx . . . 3 . . . bring on any feeling associated with the causal event and . . . 2 . . . bring it on strongly now and 1 . . . five minutes before the causative event and **zero*** (*click*) there you are . . . be there . . . see it clearly . . . see the event start to unfold . . . Intensify the feelings . . . bring them on so that you can let them all go . . .

[OR . . . at the count of three . . . reduce the emotion by half . . . 1 . . . 2 . . . 3 . . .*. . . you're frightened *because* . . . You are worried *because* . . . and so on.]

OR: Now, let's move to a deeper . . . to a more creative level of relaxation . . . there are influences below the level of consciousness that are unwelcome to you . . . bring them to consciousness – they will cease to bother you in any way . . . but at the moment they may be working in some way to protect you . . . perhaps they are unaware that your circumstances at this everyday level of reality have changed . . . with the help of subcon . . . we need to know their purpose . . . and ask subcon to provide a more immediate . . . a more appropriate . . . a more life-sustaining process for the benefit of the entire bodymind system.

As I raise and lower this arm you will go seven times more deeply into relaxation [*lower the arm*] and I call upon subcon please to provide finger signals . . . allowing this finger to rise to signify 'Yes' (index) and this finger to indicate 'No' (little finger, same hand) . . . is this yes/no response process acceptable please subcon? [*Yes*] (Carry on with the ideodynamic process . . . determining when the causal factor arose and its nature, the event experienced, something heard etc. or ask to talk to the part/parts/functions involved . . . requesting ideodynamics or vocal responses).

OR . . .call time out for yourself . . . the analyst . . . at any time by saying: Fine . . . now just relax more deeply and for the next 60 seconds . . . just relax and dream . . . and the dreamstream will bring you closer and closer to the disturbing event that created the unwelcome influences that you need to understand and eliminate from your bodymind system for ever . . . just relax and dream . . . and your thumbs will waggle to signify any disturbing event . . .

And with one eye on the thumbs . . . go to your own fingers . . . and be prepared to follow the emotional lead or revert to ideodynamics or some other tack . . . rebirthing, affect bridge, ego-state etc . . . or use a deepening or compounding process . . . for example . . . 'to help the ideodynamic response process . . . I'll hold your wrist and now ask subcon to signify acceptance of the yes/no signalling system by raising the index finger for 'yes'.

Question: May I speak with the part or parts responsible for creating the symptom which we identify at the conscious level as xxxx. And then to the client: 'On a scale of ten to zero . . . when ten represents fully awake and zero represents deeply relaxed . . . where do you feel **you** are on this scale?'

[And deepen, by any deepening process].

Now . . . I'm taking your hand and turning it palm upwards and I'm taking the name xxxx and I'm tracing it here on the palm of your hand just as you can see it in your mind, right? Now I'm going to erase it from your hand and erase it from your mind at the same time, as I stroke your hand three times . . . 1 . . . 2 . . . 3 . . .

erased from your hand
erased from your mind.

There – it's gone completely . . . now try to tell me what I erased from your hand – gone completely – can't remember, can you? Fine . . . now relax still more deeply.

Now, you can just tell your conscious mind to relax – you can instruct it – you are in charge – **open your eyes – close your eyes – now relax completely**. You can relax and it gets easier every time . . . relaxed but more creatively aware.

Now – when you relax like this, you can recall things that you probably thought were lost in your memory . . . **they are not lost in your memory** . . . they may be *repressed* from your memory but they are stored for all time in your powerhouse mind . . . so I want you to go back to the first time when you were just a little child . . . on your very first day at school . . . when I click my fingers you'll be that little child on your very first day at school . . . you'll be there just as though it is happening now . . . at the count of three . . . 1 . . . 2 . . . 3 . . .* (click). There you are – you're in school . . . tell me . . . what is the teacher saying to you now? What age are you? Who is the little boy or girl sitting on your right? On your left? How do you feel about your first day at school? When I click my fingers – you'll be back in the classroom . . . tell me – do you like your teacher? What's your teacher's name? When you centre and relax . . . notice how clearly your mind functions.

When I raise and lower your arm, it will be five minutes before you first experienced the unwelcome symptoms . . . (*drop arm*) . . . tell me . . . where are you . . . indoors or outdoors . . . day or night . . . alone or with someone? Tell me . . . what's happening . . . what's being said . . . you'll know at the count of three . . . clarify the picture . . . intensify the feelings . . . and see the event unfold . . . 1 . . . 2 . . . 3 . . .* (*click*).

Bring it to consciousness . . . the scare will cease to bother you ever again . . . now . . . let's see if the same influences are involved . . . in the next event. Going forward in time to the next event at the count of three . . . 1 . . . 2 . . . 3 . . . (*). There you are . . . tell me . . . are you alone or with someone (etc).

The thumb is controlled by your inner mind . . . if anyone or anything disturbs you, that thumb will waggle and you'll be able to talk to me about it . . .

Or . . . just relax and let subcon bring to consciousness what happened and when you can talk about it your finger will rise.

In this elevated hypnotic sleep-state of mind, events of the past that have contributed directly or indirectly to your problems can be brought swiftly to mind – but not *necessarily* to your consciousness . . . but the self-limiting negative influences they have been exerting on your health and life-style can be safely vented – can be released for ever . . . you will be freed from the past and the past will be freed from you.

Going back in time now . . . going back to the event that seeded the maladaptive reaction pattern or the unwelcome symptoms . . . you'll be there as a witness of the event at the count of three . . . 1 . . . 2 . . . 3 (*). Tell me . . . what do you feel? . . . (*Anger . . . deep anger . . .*). And what else . . . what other feelings? (*I'm scared . . . ashamed . . . sad . . . whatever*).

Now multiply that feeling of shame or blame . . . let it go . . . let it vent . . . that's right . . . good! Clear it out once and for all . . . it has no validity now . . . shame is a primary affect . . . it must be cleared . . . anger is a secondary response . . . but clear that one out too . . . what would you like to say to him? . . . see him sitting there in front of you . . . and say it to him now.

Now . . . have him respond to that . . . what does **he** want to say . . . write the script . . . you're in charge.

Induction (Optional)

Prompt Sheet 8

Now – to focus your attention . . . take a long, slow deep breath and let your stomach relax and expand and just allow your eyes to close normally and naturally – and convince yourself that they're completely relaxed by testing them to make sure that they won't open . . . that's right – try to open them and convince yourself that you already know how to relax physically and now . . . send that feeling of relaxation all the way through the body . . . all the way down to your toes – and now all the way down your arms to your fingers – just stretch . . . and relax . . . all your muscles becoming lazy, limp, relaxed . . . and now go even deeper as I pick up your arm . . . and just let it relax . . . let it completely relax . . . that's better . . . feel the difference – the muscles becoming lazy, limp relaxed – and the other arm . . . beautifully relaxed. And as I lower the arm . . . double your state of relaxation . . . great . . . and now in a moment I'll ask you to open and then close your eyes and you'll go ten times deeper into relaxation – relaxed but fully aware – in fact your awareness is increasing with each breath that you take and with each suggestion I make – now, open your eyes . . . close your eyes and go ten times deeper . . . more relaxed . . . more centred . . . more fully in control – just letting go . . . taking time out for yourself – great. Now . . . once more . . . open your eyes . . . close your eyes and feel your relaxation deepening more . . . and more . . . deeper.

That's a good state of physical relaxation and you can reach it any time in the future merely by counting mentally 1 . . . 2 . . . 3 . . . relax, relax . . . while we're here working together or at any time that you choose that is appropriate to your needs of the moment – with your eyes either open or closed.

Now – to ensure mental relaxation, I'm going to ask you in a moment to count downwards from 100 . . . and as you say each number you'll automatically double your state of mental relaxation so that by the time you get to 97 . . . you'll be sixteen times more relaxed and the numbers just won't be there . . . you'll relax the other numbers right out of your thoughts . . . you will be mentally relaxed.

So – slowly start counting from 100 . . . and double your state of relaxation . . . (100) . . . double your relaxation . . . next number . . . (99) . . . numbers starting to fade . . . try to say the next number . . . (98) . . . double your state of relaxation and try to say the next number . . . (97) . . . double your state of relaxation . . . and the numbers are all gone. Numbers all gone? Good.

Now – there's a person, place or event that links to the very first time the sensitivity that gave birth to your problem was created and in a moment – when I reach forward and tap your forehead – the word will spring to mind – the person, place or event that helped to create your problem . . . at the count of three . . . (tap) . . . what's the word?
   [OR: There's a feeling associated with your present problem and at the count of three . . . I'm going to ask subcon to bring on that feeling so that you can describe it to me clearly . . . 1 . . . 2 . . . 3 . . .*. Now – there's the feeling – accentuate it . . . what's the feeling (and take it back to the initial sensitising event)].

Way back, something happened that you have either forgotten or thought you had cleared emotionally . . . fact is that it has been pushed to the back of your mind and you've been directing vital life-energy to keeping it there ever since . . . rather like pushing a beach ball deep into the water . . . except you don't know you're doing it . . . the feeling of tension has become your way of life . . . mental civilwar rules.

So we need to identify the initial sensitising event and restore healthy balance to your lifestyle . . . and we can achieve that if we allow subcon to do its work without interference from the monkey-mind – simply by applying process . . . or rather . . . initiating process and you've already done that – you have recognised that you have a problem . . . so great . . . now you have to ensure that you can relax and get your head . . . your conditioned mind . . . out of the way – so let's do that and you'll be amazed at the power of your own mind – it will all come easy to you.

First step in the process . . . go back to a recent event when the unwanted feeling arose . . . and nod when you have the feeling.
   On a scale of zero to ten where ten represents heavy – how strong is the feeling now?

At the count of three . . . double the feeling . . . 1 . . . 2 . . . 3 . . .*

As I count you down . . . subcon will take you back to the very first time that feeling arose.

Going back in time now . . . (8) . . . younger and younger . . . (7) . . . smaller and smaller . . . back to being very, very small . . . (6) the feeling is strong . . . (5) . . . (4) . . . (3) . . . (2) . . . (1) . . . Zero . . . There you are . . . now go back to five minutes before the feeling arose and tell me – what's happening? Alone or with someone . . . etc., etc.

Now – feel yourself getting smaller and smaller again, younger and younger – and rise up above your present body and go back along the time-line before your birth . . . or to some time before the cause of your present symptoms . . . sometime before the sensitising event or emotions occurred that sowed the seed for your present problem – to a time perhaps when you felt warm – comforted – supported and sustained – you know there was such a time so – be there now . . . when you're there, your head will nod. Good . . . now – come forward in time to a few moments before the event or experience that created the sensitivity that is producing the unwelcome symptom . . .

When you're there – your right index finger will rise . . . and you'll be able to tell me about it. You're there now – just a few minutes before the causative event . . . tell me . . . where do you find yourself? Have you been born? Are you alone or with someone? . . . Intensify the feeling . . . clarify the picture at the count of three . . . 1 . . . 2 . . . 3 . . .* What's happening now?

'Nothing'.

What do you feel?

'Nothing'.

Say 'I feel nothing because' . . . and finish the sentence . . . etc.

Induction (Alternative)

Prompt Sheet 9

Just close your eyes and take a long, slow, deep breath . . . relaxing your stomach . . . and focus on the outgoing breath – now test the eye muscles for relaxation and if you have already conveyed your desire to relax to your control mind you will find that your eyes won't open – test them to make sure they won't open – that's fine – now – just let that sense of relaxation go all the way down to your toes . . . let your whole body relax . . . Now, in a moment, I'm going to ask you to open and close your eyes . . . close your eyes . . . and again . . . open your eyes . . . close your eyes and go ten times deeper into relaxation . . . releasing . . . relaxing . . . just letting go. Now, as I pick up and release your arm – you'll go still deeper into relaxation . . . feel your arm go limp – limp, loose and relaxed . . . that's great . . . that's Phase One physical relaxation and you will achieve that level of relaxation any time in the future when it is appropriate just by saying . . . 1 . . . 2 . . . 3 . . . **relax** . . . **relax** . . . Phase One . . .

Now for Phase Two mental relaxation, I'll ask you in a moment to count down from 100 . . . and each time you say a number, you'll double your mental relaxation so that by the time you reach 97, the numbers will have faded away . . . you will relax the numbers right out of your thoughts. Now, start counting and watch those numbers disappear as you relax . . . count out loud please . . . (*100*). Now double your relaxation as the numbers start to fade (*99*) double your relaxation (*98*). Now let them go . . . the thoughts you don't want in your mind . . . you learn how to tell them to go. The numbers all gone? Good . . . mentally relaxed but more aware and you will find you can go back to any event in your life that has relevance to your present-day problems.

Deepening (Short Form)

Prompt Sheet 10

I'm going to ask you three questions in a moment and you will nod your head if the answer is yes . . . do you know what a telephone looks like? . . . A tree? . . . A giraffe? . . . that's visualising . . . the word conveys the picture to subcon control . . . that's all you need to do to expand your consciousness.

So . . . imagine there's a ruler standing upright out there in front of you, marked from ten to zero . . . where ten represents the fully conscious level of awareness – and with zero representing deep relaxation . . . what level would you say you are at . . . at the moment . . . from ten to zero? (6 . . . right . . . and you will reach that level immediately in future whenever you choose and whenever you or I count 1 . . . 2 . . . 3 . . . relax . . . relax . . . We'll call it Level Two . . .

Now I'll guide you to a still deeper level, to the basement level of relaxation and you will take yourself back to Level Two and then down to the basement level so that you can always do so when it is appropriate for you . . . and at that level subcon will provide a two-way communication channel to allow you to expand your self-understanding and clear any self-limiting negative influences or repressed emotions, at all times of course while maintaining harmony and balance throughout the entire bodymind system.

Now – to reach the basement level of relaxation, you will require to go down one more level – to Level Three. As you go down, you will double your state of relaxation . . . so that by the time you reach Level Three . . . you will be beautifully relaxed . . . creatively relaxed . . . and you can go to any event in your life and be there or experience it again as a witness . . . to any event that will help you to resolve your present problems.

Deepening (Elman/Esdaile State)

Prompt Sheet 11

The art of relaxing at will – whatever the circumstances – is the key to successful living – to a healthy, rewarding lifestyle. It's a knack – learn it once, it works for you spontaneously from then on . . . and that's what I'm going to show you . . . how to relax . . . creatively . . . [because the client is still uptight . . . breathing control . . . relaxed stomach . . . any concern at the moment? . . . I'll show you how to take time out for yourself . . . simple countdown].

Now . . . go to a time in your life when you felt really happy and relaxed . . . a holiday time if you like . . . and when you're there in your thoughts, give your head a nod [elaborate as necessary].

Great . . . now pick a keyword that will always trigger the memory of that time in your thoughts . . . the name of a person, place, date or event . . . whatever will remind you of that moment. Good . . . now, as you mentally repeat the word – make a fist and then relax your hand – anchor the word to the feeling.

Now – I'll say the word . . . xxxx . . . how does that feel? Good . . . and as I lift and release your arm . . . you double that feeling of relaxation. **Now you've got it!** . . . Feel the difference? That's physical relaxation . . . Phase One . . . and with each breath that you take . . . just allow yourself to go deeper . . . and enjoy. Any time in the future when it is appropriate or while we're working together . . . you will respond to the keyword . . . xxxx . . . by relaxing to a more creative level of relaxation.

So, see yourself now in a department store or a shopping mall . . . one that you know or invent one if you like . . . make it bright and modern and you're on Floor D and you walk over to the escalator to take you down to Floor C . . . now step onto the escalator and feel it carrying you down . . . down . . . down . . . doubling your state of relaxation . . . and try to say the floor letter out loud . . . Good . . .

37

Now, walk around to the escalator to take you down to the next floor
– step on . . . now go drifting down, doubling your state of relaxation
. . . and again, try to say the floor letter out loud . . . and now on
down to the basement level of relaxation . . . to the lower floor . . .
step onto the escalator again and double your state of relaxation as
you drift down . . . down . . . down . . . feel yourself becoming deeply
relaxed. Now – try to raise one of your legs . . . good, now stop trying
and relax even more.

Now – try to open your eyes . . . good . . . that's an excellent state
of creative relaxation . . . you'll be surprised how easy it is to go to
any event in your life that will stimulate your self-understanding . . .
that will stimulate the healing process.

[Comment]
This level is usually excellent for precision therapy . . . or you can
ask subcon to move the client to a suitable working level or deepen
the state by going down another floor to the sub-basement . . . and
(at the possible risk of creating, in some people, a great reluctance to
come back) . . .
'As you reach the sub-basement – you see in front of you the symbol
for zero – outlined by light . . . and you walk through to the other
side of zero – the plus side of zero and *for a moment* be fully in touch
with yourself – with your real self.'

Now – back you come . . . back to the everyday side of zero . . . still
deeply relaxed, and move to a more comfortable, a more suitable
working level to deal effectively with your presenting problem and
any other disharmony in the bodymind system.

And whenever it is appropriate to ensure your vibrant good
health and wellbeing, you will reach this creative level of relaxation
at any time in the future whenever you or I repeat . . . '1 . . . 2 . . . 3 . . .
relax . . . relax . . . basement', and the two-way communication channel will be cleared to enhance your life understanding . . . for your
own benefit – and for the benefit of all.

[Comment]
*Here move to establish ideodynamic responses, or create an affect bridge,
call up a word, a sentence, a symbol of the causal event or use whatever
other process is indicated. In dealing with younger children, this, or the
earlier amnesia technique can be used to induce deep sleep and the child's
history can be rewritten from conception, installing healthy concepts and,
as usual, cancelling all self-limiting negative influences.*

Link & Connect

Prompt Sheet 12

There is a feeling you have that is self-limiting in many ways . . . and we need to know what caused that feeling to arise in the first place . . . at one time it was probably understandable and even appropriate . . . it is neither of these now. So I want you to bring on that feeling now, and as I count down to zero . . . let it grow . . . let the feeling grow . . . 8 . . . 7 . . . 6 . . . let the feeling start to grow . . . 5 . . . 4 . . . 3 . . . let the feeling of (whatever) come on really strongly . . .

Feel it start to surge through every nerve . . . and cell . . . and system of your body . . . that feeling of (whatever) at its very worst.

2 . . . let it take control for a moment – you will find it can be cancelled just as easily . . . 1 . . . at the count of zero . . . you are back five minutes before that feeling first arose . . . zero. You're there now – tell me – what's happening? Where do you find yourself? Is it night or day? Indoors or outdoors? Alone or with someone?

You'll know at the count of three . . . 1 . . . 2 . . . 3 . . .*

[OR] Zero. When I tap your forehead, a word will spring to mind . . . and the word will link to the cause of the problem.

(*Tap*) . . . What's the word? I'll click my fingers and you'll say a sentence that uses the word . . .* What's the sentence? Now – take that sentence and the feeling back to the very **first** time the feeling came – at the count of three . . . 1 . . . 2 . . . 3 . . .*

[OR go back – smaller and smaller – younger and younger, etc.]

Then . . . go to the next time, etc.

Negative Responses

Prompt Sheet 13

Dealing with 'nothing' responses . . .
Make a choice – what are you experiencing now?
Nothing.
I'm going to touch your forehead and at the third tap – you'll go to
another time that links to your problem. Where are you now?
Nowhere – I see nothing.
Good – so talk to me about nothing. We start from nothing anyway
. . . say . . . 'I can see nothing because . . .'
Because I can't.
Describe to me what it feels like to be nothing. Start: 'I'm nothing . . .'
and complete a sentence.
I'm nothing – I never am.
Where does that feeling come from . . . choose a part of you that has
the feeling.
Have that part talk to your head . . . (your heart) . . . and say 'I'm the
(whatever) . . .' and finish the sentence.

Now . . . at the count of zero . . . go to another time that involved that
feeling . . . 3 . . . 2 . . . 1 . . . zero . . .*
Where are you now? Quickly.

How old are you? . . . Older than 10? . . .
Older than 5? . . .
What age are you? . . .
What's going on? . . .

Where are you now? 'I don't know.' You'll know when I touch your
hand. Where are you in your thoughts? 'Nowhere.' How do you
experience nowhere – what's the feeling? 'Emptiness.' Where do
you feel that emptiness? 'In my stomach.' Be your stomach for a
moment – give it a voice. Start: 'I am the stomach and I feel empty

40

because . . .' finish the sentence. 'Because I get frightened.' Because you feel frightened. Fine. Let's follow that along a bit. Let's find how the feeling originated. After all, there must have been a start to it. I'll count down from three . . . and you'll go all the way back along the past timeline to the very first time you had the feeling of fright. Right . . . counting 3 . . . intensify the feeling . . . 2 . . . going back now, through the years and taking the feeling with you . . . 1 . . . younger and younger . . . smaller and smaller . . . to the very first time that feeling came . . . and zero . . . you're there . . . the very first time and tell me . . . where are you now? . . . quickly . . . indoors or outdoors? Night or day? Alone or with someone? Now – be there and report what's happening. Are you younger than ten? Than five?

And, again, dealing with nothing responses . . . Make a choice. What are you experiencing now? 'Nothing.' Now, I'm going to touch your forehead and at the third tap you'll go to another time that links to your problem. Where are you now? 'I'm nowhere – I can see nothing.' Talk to me about nothing – after all, we all start from nothing. 'I can see nothing because . . .' 'Because I can't.' Describe to me what it feels like to be nothing. Start: 'I'm nothing' and complete the sentence. 'I'm nothing – I never am.' Where does that feeling come from? Choose a part of you that has that feeling. Talk to your head (your heart) and say: 'I'm the [whatever] and . . .' finish the sentence. Now at the count of zero, go to an earlier time that involved that feeling . . . 3 . . . 2 . . . 1 . . . zero . . .* Where are you now? Quickly . . . how old are you? Are you older than ten? Older than five? What's going on?

Where are you now? 'I don't know.' You'll know when I touch your hand . . . where are you in your thoughts? 'Nowhere.' How do you experience nowhere? . . . what's the feeling? 'Emptiness.' Where do you feel that emptiness? 'In my stomach.' Be your stomach for a moment – give it a voice . . . start: 'I'm the stomach and I feel empty because . . .' . . . finish the sentence. 'Because I get frightened.' . . . Because you feel frightened . . . fine . . . let's follow that feeling along a bit more . . . let's find how the feeling originated . . . after all . . . there must have been a first time.

I'll count down from 3 and you'll go all the way back along the past timeline to the very first time you had the feeling of fright . . . counting (3) . . . intensify the feeling . . . let it really grow . . . (2) . . . going back now, through the years and taking the feeling with you . . . (1) . . . younger and younger . . . smaller and smaller . . . to the very first time that feeling came and zero . . .* (click) you're there . . .

the very first time . . . and tell me . . . where are you now? Quickly . . .
indoors or outdoors . . . night or day . . . alone or with someone . . . be
there . . . and report what's happening . . .

Are you younger than ten? . . . than five? . . . what age are you?

Every breath that you take is taking you to a deeper level of awareness . . . tell me . . . where are you now? . . . What do you feel?
'Nothing.'
Let's see if your inner mind agrees. I'll ask subcon to put your thumb
[this one] under its control . . . it will waggle each time subcon
knows that the responses you are giving are incomplete in any way.

. . . What do you have in your thoughts now?
'Nothing . . .'

Open your eyes . . . look at your thumb . . . now – close your eyes and
go seven times more deeply into relaxation as I count you down
from six to zero . . . there's something that is creating disharmony in
the bodymind system that you need to know . . . and I'll ask subcon
on your behalf to ensure that all levels of mind and being are
cooperating fully in releasing whatever information will restore
harmony and balance to the entire bodymind system now . . . as I am
here to act as part of the healing process . . . and to do so as I count
down from six to zero . . . counting 6 . . . going back in time now – to
fifteen minutes before the event that created the unwelcome symptoms . . . 5 . . . the event will come clearly to mind . . . 4 . . . your
awareness increases with each breath that you take . . . 3 . . . 2 . . . 1
. . . zero . . .*. **There you are now**.

Ideomotor Responses and Ego-States

Prompt Sheet 14

Ask subcon if there is a level of mind or being that is locked into responding to emotions or events in some outdated or obsolete way. May I communicate with the part or function vocally? Through the means of finger signals? I will refer to the part or function at the moment as Part X and explain that I am part of John Willy's healing process . . . and I appreciate that Part X has a positive purpose in behaving in this way . . . and I would like to know what it is and how Part X can apply it to more creative, constructive and life-enhancing purpose . . . I can assure Part X that this can be done with the help of subcon . . .

Part X . . . do you have a name?

Am I right in thinking you have a positive purpose? Is the purpose to [*here, call on your own subcon to provide you with a theme to develop. Whatever the negative side is, see the positive possibility and continue from there to resolve the problem . . . or . . . chat with subcon . . . as follows:*]

Can you explain to Part X that its actions are inappropriate and outdated – are, in fact, creating considerable disharmony and problems . . . can you do so now, please?

Can you provide Part X with three more creative options – with three more immediate, more appropriate, more life-enhancing processes for achieving its aims for the benefit of the entire bodymind system – including, of course, itself please?

Has the part accepted one of these options?

Can it do so now please and see how it works over the next few weeks, substituting a still more beneficial alternative if the need arises etc., etc., including: subcon notify beneficial changes in behavioural patterns for implementation by the conscious levels of mind as required through the medium of dreams and experiences.

Deepening Technique: Confusion

Prompt Sheet 15

(Close eyes) **Try/test them . . . see . . . you can relax your eye muscles!** Now I'd like you to try to stay very alert . . . try to avoid letting your thoughts drift for I know you can relax when you need to for the benefit of the entire bodymind system and your conscious mind will have very little or nothing to do with it . . . I know you have a vast array of resources available to you that your conscious mind is completely unaware of – in fact you have the ability to surprise yourself . . .

Somewhere in your personal history you have resources available . . . you have potential for excellence in every phase of your being and sometimes it's pleasant just to sit back and relax, take time out for yourself, letting your bodymind system relax and enjoy and as you listen to me and concentrate just on what is being said you will acquire new choices, new behavioural patterns, new self- understanding and awareness for there are times you can be aware of certain thoughts and feelings and at other times you may be unaware of them in fact you are unaware most of the time which is a kind of relaxation but the kind you need to develop is relaxation with enhanced awareness . . . for example continue to try not to relax and become aware of the feeling of your feet in your shoes – after all, at the conscious levels of mind you will find it impossible to remember the future or project yourself forward into the past and it may be enough to sit and think about where you were at this time yesterday or last year but memory always distorts and we want clear pictures of events in your life and that is the sole province of the subconscious control levels of mind – your powerhouse or treasurehouse mind.

And you may find it easy to let your thoughts drift to another time or place – perhaps to a place out in nature – choose a place you know or invent one if you like – and make it a glorious summer day . . .

introduce a holiday feeling . . . feel how pleasant it is to daydream . . . to relax . . . release . . . to let thoughts drift . . . and bring to mind now a time when you were really sleepy . . . drowsy . . . how pleasant it was to drift off into a deep, blissful sleep and sleep deeply – deeply and soundly . . . and those are the good feelings you can feel growing stronger and stronger in you now and you can relax and you will automatically drift deeper with every breath that you take and as I count down the numbers from 8 to 1 just try to repeat the numbers after me and double your state of relaxation as you follow the shape of the numbers with your eyes comfortably closed as I count 8 . . . (try to say the number) . . . 7 (try to say the number) . . . deeper into relaxation . . . 6 . . . going down now . . . 5 . . . down . . . down . . . down . . . 4 . . . time out to relax . . . 3 . . . time out to enjoy . . . 2 . . . yet becoming more aware . . . more fully in control . . . 1 . . . drifting down now to zero . . . zero . . . zero . . . to a pleasant working level of creative relaxation.

Elman Pinpointing

Prompt Sheet 16

Going back to your birthday at the age of ten . . . there you are now . . . at the age of ten . . . tell me . . . what presents do you have? It's your tenth birthday. Now . . . you're ten years old . . . do you know what a headache is like? (*Yes*).

Now, let's go back to the age of five. It's your fifth birthday . . . 1 . . . 2 . . . 3 . . .* there you are . . . does a little child of five know what a headache is like? (*No*).

So . . . somewhere between the ages of five and ten your headache was caused . . . some emotional event occurred . . . and you are reliving that event over and over at a level below consciousness. When I touch your forehead – you'll be there again . . . fifteen minutes before the event that created the headache . . . there you go . . . see the event unfold . . . tell me . . . where are you now? Indoors or outdoors . . . night or day . . . alone or with someone?

Now, let's ask subcon through the medium of finger signals if that was the sensitising event.

[*Then go forward to later events, linking to a recent event. Then ensure the need for the symptom is no longer required . . . mental, physical and emotional release . . .*].

Dreamwork

Prompt Sheet 17

So – you woke up with a headache . . . now let's see if something disturbed you emotionally while you slept.

I'll reach forward and touch your forehead and it's just as though you have switched on a television set . . . and now . . . focus on the screen and see yourself sleeping in bed . . . and (just as you have seen in a film sometimes) see the dream sequence unfolding above you on the screen as you sleep . . . it's happening now . . . and you'll see what's happening in the dream as I count slowly from three . . . to zero . . . 3 . . . see the dream . . . 2 . . . happening now . . . 1 . . . zero . . . you can see the dream . . . tell me – what's happening?

Fine . . . relax still more deeply . . . focus on the expressions on your face as you lie there . . . sleeping . . . dreaming . . . and when I click my fingers . . . you'll see a symbol that will link and connect to the nature of the dream . . . * . . . there you are . . . tell me – what do you see?

   Good . . . good . . . now, when I lift and drop your arm . . . you will know what subcon wants to convey . . . and you will know the meaning of the dream.

Testing for Behavioural Changes

Prompt Sheet 18

Now – I'd like you to move ahead in your thoughts one week . . . a week has gone by since you attended for analysis . . . a week in which you applied your deeper understanding to your day-to-day activities.

Now . . . tell me . . . looking back at those last seven days since your analysis session . . . what differences have you seen in your lifestyle?

[*This is a multi-purpose step . . . it invariably provides valuable insights into the way the client has translated your generalities into his own specifics . . . your suggestions into dealing with problems that he may not have mentioned earlier.*]

DOUBLE-CHECKING WITH IDEOMOTOR SIGNALS

Note that it is worthwhile establishing ideodynamic signalling whenever possible, if only to provide a double-check on some other types of response . . . for example . . . to question if there is any other major problem that needs to be resolved that is possibly known only to subcon . . . or to verify that all parts and functions and systems are benefiting from the release of a repression and from the establishment of new habit patterns etc. . . . . or requesting the thumbs to be placed exclusively under subcon control and to waggle if conscious understanding of any point is incorrect or incomplete or if there is conscious mind interference.

Even if the response to any one uncovering theme is poor . . . deepen the state and return to the theme again later . . . it is often found to be fully effective the second time around . . . sometimes even immediately after the first attempt has proved unfruitful.

Birth

Prompt Sheet 19

Our early negative conditioning has created our two greatest fears –
our fear of loving – and of being loved . . . our inability, for example,
to love ourselves as we are – always seeking to become – and our
inability to reveal our true feelings to anyone – even hiding them
from ourselves.

So . . . what created these repressions . . . these false feelings –
what created the barriers between you and the loving feelings of the
seedmind within? What created anger, frustration, resentment and
fear . . . you weren't born with fear and anger or self-hate and
resentment – **or were you?** Your feelings haven't been repressed
from birth – **or have they?**

This is one of the sounds you registered when your journey into
this level of consciousness began – the nearby sound of a human
heart-beat . . . with the help of subcon . . . the sound of the heart-beat
will now open a two-way channel in your consciousness to a time
before your birth, possibly even before your conception . . . and all
the birth and pre-birth experiences that are influencing your present
lifestyle will surface in your conscious awareness as the birth process unfolds – at the count of zero . . . it is sometime before your birth
. . . 3 . . . 2 . . . 1 . . . zero (*click*) . . . you can experience yourself now as
a seedcell or an embryo or a foetus . . . secure in your mother's body
. . . warmed, comforted, supported and sustained – afloat in a liquid
environment – aware of the sounds around you . . . the movements
. . . your mother's moods and feelings – if anything upsets or disturbs you – your thumbs will waggle . . . your awareness increases
moment to moment . . . be aware of how you feel . . . tell me . . . do
you want to be born? Do you want to be born?

Your mother – does she want you to be born? Your father – how
does he feel about your forthcoming birth . . . if you have brothers or
sisters . . . how do they feel about you being born? What's being

thought and said about your forthcoming birth? Your family's financial position – your father's job security – how your mother and father get on together – you know all that.

It's now a moment or two before your birth – moving along the birth canal – how do you feel – does your head seek to move to the left or the right . . . let it move when you experience the pressure of delivery . . . a contraction . . . another contraction . . . feel it . . . feel it . . . you're being born . . . pressure . . . moving . . . turning . . . feel your shoulders move . . . as soon as your head is out [**stop 'heartbeat'**] lift the shoulder that is being born first . . . the arm . . . the other shoulder . . . what's happening?

Howling . . . what's that noise? Air . . . gulping air . . . thin stuff . . . do you **want to be born . . .? How do you feel about being born?**
   [*No real need for movement or verbal responses – allow time for feelings*].

Now relax . . . relax still more deeply and review the entire birthing experience fully again – you will learn more about your reactions and feelings – learning more about your responses – do you need any assistance in being born? – your mother – is she awake or asleep? – how does she feel? Listen to what is being said – who holds you immediately you arrive? . . . when you know all you need to know and can talk to me about it, your head will nod.

You won your way into this life against the most incredible odds – the odds against were several million to one . . . and that invisible essence or energy force – Lifeforce – is the creative reality in you now. Treasure it – honour it – and **get to know it well** . . . it is your personal guide on your journey through life.

Forgiveness and the Wounded Child-Mind

Prompt Sheet 20

Wherever there is a complete healing – there must be complete forgiveness – all wounds at all levels must be healed.

How many people have the good fortune in life to become aware . . . as you have become aware . . . of the impact on your behavioural patterns of influences that were outside your conscious understanding and control?

The person who abused you was driven by these self-same unconscious forces.

There's no need to excuse that behaviour . . . but – with your new understanding . . . **can you forgive that person? Can you forgive . . . and forget? Forgive . . . forget . . . and focus – not on the past – focus on now – this ever new moment of now. Say it! . . . I forgive you Father – I am free from you . . . and you are free from me . . .**

Fine – what else do you want to do or say to your father?

Now listen . . . as I tap your forehead . . . you will hear what your father now says to you . . . (*tap*). What does he say?

What do you respond? (*Gestalt-type conversation*).

So – what have you learned from this experience?

It has guided you to find a source of great strength in yourself.

Accept – be grateful – stride on!!!

Unrelaxed

Prompt Sheet 21

Is there anything bothering you at the moment?

Now – I'd like you to answer these questions with a 'Yes' or 'No' please.

Are you interested in getting rid of the problem?

'Yes'.

Do you know how to get rid of it?

'No.'

Do you consider that I might?

'Yes.'

How can you be sure?

'I don't know.'

I do – by following my suggestions – then you can find out for yourself. Do you agree?

'Yes.'

Then – let's do that . . . follow my suggestions to the letter. OK? Yes or no?

Reluctance to Discuss or Disclose

Prompt Sheet 22

So you future-pace.

Now – there may be some level of mind that is concerned with protecting the old thinking and habit patterns – reliving old traumas, replaying old tapes – a level of mind or being unaware that it is locked into an outdated behavioural pattern . . . reliving history instead of responding appropriately to the needs of the moment.

And it may be so out of touch with ongoing living reality that it is not prepared to release its fears and apprehensions to consciousness right now. **Let me ask** . . . with increased self-understanding – can it reveal its problems in twelve months' time . . . twelve months from now? . . . Twenty-four months from now? Good!! So just relax ten times more deeply as I raise and let fall your arm . . . there you go . . . your awareness and self-understanding increasing with each breath that you take and with each suggestion I make . . . as I count . . . (6) . . . and you are creatively relaxed . . . (5) . . . a more elevated level of awareness . . . (4) . . . a healing level . . . at which you are in touch with any and all events that have relevance to your well- being . . . and . . . (3) . . . you move ahead in accelerated timeflow . . . (2) . . . you move six months ahead in time . . . twelve months . . . and at the count of zero (1) you are two years ahead in time (zero) . . . and it is now 1996 . . . and your self-understanding is incredible . . . **and** at the count of 3 . . . a word will spring to mind to link and connect to the cause of your problem . . . 1 . . . 2 . . . 3 . . . * . . . there you are . . . tell me the word . . . quickly . . . what is the word? Good . . . now – link the word to the cause . . . you will see the cause . . . you will see the cause . . . bring it clearly to mind . . . release the emotion (*). Report to me . . . tell me what is happening in consciousness.

[*Later – back to now*]

And later still:

You really surprised yourself there didn't you? (*To confirm that they were not conscious memories*).

Enhanced Coping Skills

Prompt Sheet 23

Now that you've discovered the source of your problem and seen how it links to later reinforcing events and experiences . . . is there any need for you to respond in that way?

What internal resources do you need besides understanding to ensure that you will not only succeed in the future . . . you will excel?

Sense of direction . . . justifiable self-confidence . . . competence and courage . . . **enhanced coping skills**.

Now – go back to a time in the past when you called your coping skills into play and you succeeded.

Nod your head when you're there.

Good . . . now pick a keyword to remind you of that event . . . the name of a person, place or thing. Got it? What's the word?

Now – as you repeat the word . . . make a fist . . . anchor the feeling . . . and then relax. Keyword . . . anchor the feeling . . . be there – feel it . . . then relax . . . great.

Now . . . I'll paint you a scene that, in the past, would perhaps have disturbed you . . . only this time and in the future, as you mentally repeat and anchor the keyword . . . you will eliminate all self-limiting negative influences.

And I'd like you, from your more elevated vantage point, to elaborate on the scene I will paint in words. (*Here describe an event that would have disturbed the client – ensuring that he is using the anchoring process*) . . . Now – how did you feel about that? 'Good' . . . and soon, that will become a conditioned response – a healthy conditioned response – you will not only succeed – you will do better than well . . . you will excel.

Now – you know what caused your problem and you know what compounded it – a sensitivity was created by the initial event and everything that seemed to have the same or a similar emotional content served to strengthen the sensitivity . . . and now that you know how it all happened, is there any need for you to keep responding in the same way?

'No – I don't think so.'

That's what you don't think . . . what do you know about your coping skills . . . are they the same as those you had as a three-year-old girl?

'No.'

They're different because . . . and finish the sentence.
'Because I'm not three years old now.'
That's what you're **not** . . .
Things are different now because . . .?
    'Because . . .'
Because I'm a **big girl now** . . . right?
Fix on that . . . as you close and open your fist . . . good . . . let's hear you say it.

Now . . . it's some time in the future and the sort of event occurs that, in the past, would have triggered the unwelcome response . . . but from now onwards . . . the thought will immediately flash to mind 'I'm a big girl now' . . . and you'll smile and cope with the situation – you'll take it all in your stride.

And . . . a note to subcon: 'big girl' in the sense of big in life-understanding.

Induce Feeling

Prompt Sheet 24

Now, there's bound to be a feeling associated with your problem . . . otherwise the problem simply wouldn't exist . . . are you consciously aware of the feeling you get?

'No . . .'

OK . . . so we need to bring it to consciousness and . . . at the count of three . . . to ask subcon to make you fully aware of what the feeling is and where it's coming from . . . to bring it on quite strongly so that you are aware of it and can tell me about it – the feeling associated with (whatever) – be aware of where you feel it at the count of three . . . 1 . . . 2 . . . 3 . . . *.

Where is the feeling . . . indicate it to me.

Now – to confirm that this is how your body physically reflects the problem – I'll ask subcon to intensify the feeling for a moment at the count of three . . . 1 . . . 2 . . . 3 . . . *.

What happened . . . You got the feeling more strongly?

Now – let's take that feeling back to the very first time . . . the very first time as I count you back in time from six to zero . . . going back to that very first time.

Private Therapy

Prompt Sheet 25

Just close your eyes as I touch your shoulder **and as we breathe together in unison go deeply asleep** . . . (*touch shoulder*). Deeper . . . with each breath that you take . . . (*raise arm . . . straighten . . . tap arm downwards. . .*). I will call your problem Problem X . . . because it may not even be a conscious one . . . it will be something . . . that is limiting your lifestyle in some way or another.

As I tap your forehead . . . a word or phrase will spring to mind . . . it will link your consciousness to the problem.

(*Tap. . .*)

Nod when you have received the word or phrase.
(*Nods*)

Focus on the word or phrase for a moment
. . . I'll raise and drop your hand.
As your hand drops . . . you will see
the solution to your problem.
(*Raise and drop hand*).
Nod when the solution is clear.

(*Nods*)

I'll click my fingers and you'll be fully awake with a smile on your face and a song in your heart (*).

Tell me – what's the song in your heart?

Would you like to talk to me about what happened?

Oh . . . you've lost that relaxation for a moment.

Now . . . It's one thing being able to relax after strenuous physical exercise . . . it's another thing being able to relax at will at a mental/emotional level . . . to relax creatively. Let me show you how to do that whenever you choose.

To relax your hand – you stretch out the fingers – then you stop stretching . . . relaxation happens all by itself. To relax mentally . . . you focus on something . . . then you stop focussing . . . it's as easy as that.

So open your eyes wide . . . look upwards . . . and close your eyes and feel the eye-muscles relax . . . notice how good it feels . . .

Now – focus your thoughts on your feet . . . (*and go through the round-the-body sequence . . . hands . . . shoulders . . . lips . . . tongue*).

Now test yourself for relaxation.

Try to raise one of your legs . . . try really hard . . . now stop trying and **really relax**.

Now this time as I touch your forehead in the area of the pineal gland . . . a name of a person – a place – an event or a thing will immediately spring to mind . . . it will link and connect your consciousness to something that is a problem to you . . . a problem that subcon will then resolve.

1 . . . 2 . . . 3 . . . (*tap*).

There you are . . . what's the word?

As I click my fingers you'll know what the problem is (*click*).

Intensify the image (*click*).

Now you know the problem.

Now – go to the solution . . . 1 . . . 2 . . . 3 . . . *.

Bring it clearly to mind.

Nod your head when you are ready to talk.

Deepening

Prompt Sheet 26

Now place the symbol for zero out there in front of you and make it big enough for you to float right through it to the other side – to the passive side of zero. Great! . . . and experience a sense of eternal bliss . . . of unlimited power . . . the sense of restoraton and renewal . . . go there from time to time to recharge your mental, emotional and physical batteries, coming back in your own time . . . because, of course, that's the only time there is.

There is no eternal past leading to an eternal future . . . life isn't a dress-rehearsal for something else . . . life is an eternal moment of now . . . each moment is yours to choose . . . yours to enjoy.

So . . . for a moment . . . choose to enjoy . . . become one with the stillness . . . the creative power of your own treasurehouse mind . . . from which all things manifest . . . choose to enjoy . . .*.

Now . . . come gently back to this side of zero . . . and notice how deeply relaxed and aware you are . . . you can go to any event in your life that has relevance to your needs of the moment. So let's ask subcon control to provide you with a 'Yes/No' signalling system that you can use now . . . the centre of truth in yourself.

Four Life Needs

Prompt Sheet 27

So let us see where you stand in fulfilling your four greatest needs
. . . and if there are others . . . you will bring them to mind and tell me
about them . . . so what are the four needs common to all human-
kind?

There's the need to act and succeed.

The need to assert yourself appropriately.

The need to look forward with hope.

The need for affection, comfort and respect.

How do you feel about your ability to succeed . . . to find fulfilment
in life through what you choose to do?

Do you feel confident in asserting yourself?

How do you view your future?

How about the need for affection, comfort and respect?

*(And so on . . . to ensure all hang-ups are dealt with . . . using the
anchoring process or reframing to deal with limitations).*

And now you know where to go for the answers . . . the only place
where you can find the answers for you . . . so make it a practice to
tune in to yourself from time to time – at least once during the day –
tuning in to life – not tuning out . . . becoming more and more aware
of the options that life offers . . . they are being offered to you every
moment of every day. *(And ask subcon if there is any other important
need).*

Redirecting Energy

Prompt Sheet 28

If (2) for green on the Lüscher scale is in the last three, you can use this theme:

Your energy level is very low – low resilience and linked with that is an inability to assert yourself – right?

Yet your life-energy is just as strong as anyone else's – you're just directing it to suppress old emotions – and the more you do that, the more of your strength – the more of your psychic energy – you give to negativity – you feed it your strength and it comes back for more!

The negativity must be recognised – and released. It's history now.

Do you know what a transformer is?

It's a gadget that transforms electrical energy – so that we can direct it to creative purpose.

That's what I'm going to show you how to do with Lifeforce – to reverse the polarity and apply your energy to creative purpose . . . to health . . . to living, laughing, loving and learning . . . to enjoying every new moment of now.

A very negative person will claim that they feel that life isn't worth living.

What they are saying, of course, is that they have not found how to live with their thoughts – they've found themselves unworthy of life.

Cease acting as judge and jury on yourself.

'You can't help me' translates to 'I don't consider myself worthy of your help'.

Accept that correction – you can be helped . . . easily . . . we're all being helped all the time . . . we're all deserving of help.

You've learned to attract problems . . . quite unconsciously – now you're going to learn to cease doing that: that's all. We're going to apply a simple universal law . . . we're going to reverse polarity . . . you've been seeking outside yourself for answers . . . I'm going to show you how to look in the right place . . . instead of seeking outside for answers . . . to seek inside – to seek who's seeking . . . to seek the seeker! Finding the seeker, you find answers to all the problems in the world . . . you see . . . you've been educated away from your nature . . . now you'll find your way back. What's the secret in hypnosis? The secret is so obvious . . . we miss it, we're like fishes trying to find out what water is. The secret of hypnosis is that it is our natural state . . . it's what makes us human beings. We live in a mental and emotional state of unconscious self-hypnosis . . . until we become conscious of it . . . through practising conscious self-hypnosis . . . then you recognise the state!

There is a material reality . . . hot is hot and cold is cold . . . heat can burn . . . our unconscious hypnosis is that we carry the memory of the burn into the new moment of now. We relive the memory mentally – often at a level below consciousness. We keep the burn alive!! That's unconscious self-hypnosis.

We can limit ourselves in millions of ways . . . we fail to experience living reality . . . we crowd out the present with the ghosts of past experiences . . . you're going to learn how to drop all self-limiting negative illusions . . . to stop the past obscuring the present. When you cease living and reliving the past . . . you live in the now . . . the ever-new moment of now . . . you start living life . . . you cease reliving history.

Ego-State Process

Prompt Sheet 29

Subcon . . . to assist in John's healing process, I'd like to know if there is a part of John that has dissociated itself from the rest of the bodymind system for some reason . . . if another 'ego state' exists . . . (*Yes*) I would like to speak to that part and when it can speak to me . . . please have it say 'I'm here' (*I'm here*). Thank you part . . . my name is Duncan and I'm part of John's healing process – do you have a name please? (*Grey*). Thank you Grey . . . how old was John when you came into being? (*Six years old*). So something happened which made it necessary for you to come into being – can you explain to me now please what happened? (*Explanation given*).

So you have been seeking to help John by . . . *describe what has been happening and then redefine the objective in positive terms . . . then ask subcon to provide two more acceptable alternatives . . . have the part select one for implementation etc . . . for the benefit of the entire bodymind system . . . and ensure that all parts, functions and systems are now happy with the new behavioural pattern . . . and it will be modified, adjusted and improved from time to time with the help of subcon whenever necessary to meet the specific needs of the moment in a constructive, creative and life-enhancing way.*

Alternative approach:

I'd like to ask subcon if there is a part of the bodymind system that is responsible for producing the symptom or effect . . .

(*Yes*) . . .

I appreciate that the part is performing what may seem to it to be an essential function but it must be getting tired of its role . . . I assure it that it has the capability for so much more creative purpose. I'd like to talk to it about that . . . can the part respond to me now please as part of John's healing function by saying 'I'm ready Duncan'?

Do you have a name, part? (Then I'll call you Part X).

My understanding, subject to correction, Part X, is that you dissociated when something happened to him/her in the past . . . is this correct?

What age was he/she when this happened?

What actually happened?

So, you have been trying to (safeguard, comfort, protect) him/her (*see a positive reason for the action*).

Explain the effect on lifestyle and offer a better alternative and ask subcon's help (if necessary, on a trial basis).

Thank all functions and subcon.

How do you feel now that Part X is working with you in harmony and balance?

This sense of oneness – of wholeness . . . will further expand and grow . . . all levels of mind and body will now and in the future coordinate to ensure spontaneous right action.

Attenuating Emotions

Prompt Sheet 30

Now, go forward in your imagination to a situation that would have caused you apprehension in the past and if we have cleared out all the feelings of fear . . . you will be able to go through the situation quite comfortably . . . go forward now . . . and nod to me when you have gone right through the situation.

Have all the uncomfortable feelings gone completely?

'Nearly.'

All right . . . so there is something there that still needs to be cleared . . . focus on the feeling and as I count you down to zero let the feeling grow . . . as I count 6 . . . be aware of the unwelcome feeling . . . 5 . . . intensify it so that all levels of being are aware of it . . . 4 . . . you want to know how it is caused . . . 3 . . . the feeling growing stronger now . . . as you go back to fifteen minutes before the first time it arose . . . 2 . . . you'll be there at the count of zero . . . 15 minutes before the event . . . 1 . . . nearly there . . . you'll see the event unfold . . . zero . . . **there** you are . . . tell me . . . is it night or day . . . etc.

Intensify the feeling . . . clarify the picture . . . as I click my fingers (*) there you are . . . what's happening to you?

You're feeling that way because . . . ?

I'll touch your hand and you'll be there . . . you'll report to me.

Bringing the event to consciousness it will cease to trouble you from now on . . . it will lose its self-limiting negative impact . . . you will be free from the past . . . you will cease reliving history. At the count of three . . . tell me . . . what's the feeling? . . . 1 . . . 2 . . . 3 . . . (*).

(*Then, attenuate it – go through the event again, ego boost, anchor positive responses to the initial sensitising event*).

Thumb Waggle

Prompt Sheet 31

I'd like this thumb to represent awareness below the level of consciousness . . . and I'd like it to be under the control of your inner mind . . . your subconscious control mind . . . so that you are unable to waggle it consciously . . . and I'll ask you to try and waggle it . . . try really hard . . . that's right – now cease trying – know that it is under the control of subcon while we are working together for the benefit of your entire bodymind system and want subcon to convey understanding to all levels of mind . . . to guide you to the cause of your problem . . . for it is something that is bothering you – influencing your behaviour and lifestyle – at a level below consciousness and it needs to be understood . . . it represents unfinished psychic business that needs to be completed . . . allowing you to direct all your energies to more constructive, creative and life-sustaining purpose. If any of your responses are incomplete or incorrect . . . the thumb will waggle – things that you perhaps didn't even notice consciously. (*Continue questioning*).

Now, I'm going to have you open your eyes . . . see what's happening to that thumb.

So there is something more that we need to know.

Whenever you get that feeling again . . . whenever something happens that would – in the past – have triggered the unwelcome response . . . you will bring a flash of the causal event to mind . . . you will spontaneously see the original sensitising event – the cause – and the influence will cease to have power over you.

Now – I'll reach forward and tap you on the forehead . . . each time I touch your forehead, a letter of the alphabet will spring to mind – the letters will spell a word . . . a name . . . a description of a person or a place that was involved in creating your problem . . . and you will recognise the connection

    . . . 1 . . . 2 . . . 3 . . . (*tap*) the first letter
    . . . 1 . . . 2 . . . 3 . . . (*tap*) the second letter
What's the word? Now . . . see the connection (*).

66

Forgiveness

Prompt Sheet 32

Forgive and forget because . . .? You've suffered injustice . . . abuse . . . all yesterday's mashed potatoes. History. If the memory arises . . . cancel it . . . you endured it once . . . that's history . . . it has no place in your everyday living reality.

Let it clear from your mind . . . so that your options in life are more clearly visible . . . and new options are being offered to you every minute of every day . . . you need to be **open** to see them . . . to receive them . . . awake . . . and aware. If you're sending out ill-thoughts . . . you're on the wrong channel for health and happiness.

At the superficial emotional levels . . . you respond to other people's conditioning . . . you see only *their* conditioning.

At the deeper levels . . . you know we are all the same . . . we have unlimited creative potential.

You have a great opportunity to develop yours!

Accept – be grateful . . . and now . . . move on.

Be open to change . . . not change for the sake of change . . . but change because life is a process of change and renewal . . . and you're a part of it . . . not apart from it.

Go deep . . . and be renewed.

The unmindful are ruled by their conditioning – they fail to rule their personal universe . . . you will rule from within.

Initiating Process

Prompt Sheet 33

Make a presentation to a group of twenty people, perhaps ten of them will ask . . . *but supposing you had a situation in which such and such happened?* . . . and if you asked them, they could each give you a dozen ways in which they think the hypno-analysis process wouldn't work. And they're right . . . it won't work for them . . . it works for me simply because I don't think about it now . . . I know it works because I know it works. How did I get to be like that? Here's the laugh . . . because in the beginning it came right even when I thought the process was daft . . . I just used the process. Then there was a time when I collected processes . . . dozens of processes . . . and some of the early ones that worked well, stopped working well.

Why? Because my monkey-mind was focused on showing the client all the smart ways I had of doing things instead of using any one process whole-heartedly. I had what I called my 'funk-holes' . . . NLP and other show-biz-type techniques, to impress the client when the effective healing processes were not properly worked through.

Then I learned that if the response to establishing ideodynamic signalling was poor – deepen the state or move to another . . . and then ask subcon to establish ideodynamic signalling another way, perhaps as I hold the wrist . . . the second or third time, the signalling works – effortlessly!

What comes through in healing is your intention.

My intention is to excel.

(Nearly) Elman Relaxation Techniques

Prompt Sheet 34

Let me take your hand for a moment – and let it relax . . . (*ensure relaxation*).

Now take a long slow deep breath and focus on the outgoing breath . . . slowly now . . . and now another and let your tummy relax and expand.

Now, close your eyes and let the tiny muscles around the eyes relax and when you're sure that they're relaxed . . . just test them and make sure that your eyes won't open . . . (*if they open – tell the client to relax them to the extent that they just won't work – bypassing his critical mind effectively . . . accepting your suggestions and beginning to pretend*).

Notice how good you feel with that little bit of relaxation . . . and you will find that you can relax still more deeply . . . you will become **creatively** relaxed . . . tuning in rather than dropping out – and let that feeling of relaxation spread all the way down to your toes . . . pleasantly relaxed . . . each breath taking you deeper and deeper . . . but to a higher mental and emotional ventage point . . . creatively relaxed.

Now you're going to find this very interesting. In a moment I will ask you to open and close your eyes gently . . . and as you do so . . . you will go ten times more deeply relaxed . . . and every nerve and cell and system of the body will become more relaxed.

Now – gently open your eyes – and close them and relax ten times more deeply . . . good. And once again . . . open . . . close . . . and double your state of relaxation.

And again – open – close – double your state of relaxation.

Now when I drop your hand . . . it will just plop down onto your lap and you'll be completely relaxed . . .

And now I'll raise the other arm – that's wonderful . . . lazy, limp and relaxed . . . a wonderful state of physical relaxation that you can achieve yourself at any time in the future when it is appropriate with your eyes either open or closed just by saying 1 . . . 2 . . . 3 . . . relax . . . relax.

And now, when you mentally relax in a moment, you will feel a hundred times more relaxed than you do now . . . and all you have to do when I ask you in a moment is to start counting slowly backwards from one hundred . . . and each time you say a number, just double your state of relaxation . . . so that by the time you get to 97 . . . the numbers just won't be there – you'll have relaxed them right out of your thoughts . . . they will have no importance to you at the moment . . . so . . . just relax . . . say the first number . . . double your rleaxaton . . . and feel what happens . . . '100' . . . now double your relaxation and find the numbers are fading away . . . but try to say the next number.

'99' . . . now double your relaxation and when you say the next number . . . the numbers will be all gone.

'98' . . . numbers all gone . . . try to see the next number . . . all gone! Just let every breath take you deeper . . . and notice how good you feel!

[*Keep counting*] . . . Now, I'll pick up and drop your hand – as I drop it . . . let the numbers drop out of your thoughts . . . there they go . . . and now you're physically and mentally relaxed . . . **great**.

Age Regression to the Initial Causative Event

Prompt Sheet 35

(*Repeat the client's words*). Right – so you're four years old . . . it's night-time . . . you're alone . . . you're in your bedroom . . . tell me now . . . tell me . . . what's happening now?

Now . . . at the count of three . . . go to another time when you had similar feelings . . .
    1 . . . 2 . . . 3 . . . (*) there you are . . . tell me what's happening now. Indoors or outdoors . . . night or day . . . alone or with someone.

Infancy
. . . All right now . . . you're an infant child
    . . . Tell me . . . do you love your mother?
    . . . Does your mother love you?
    . . . Do you have brothers and sisters (*same theme*).

Gestalt:
This time . . . when I click my fingers . . . your father is going to be standing six feet in front of you (*). There he is . . . what do you call your father . . . Dad? (*Yes*) . . .
    All right . . . I want you to talk to him right now.
    I want you to say to him 'Dad . . . there are some things I want to ask you and I want a straight answer . . .'
    Say that to him in your own words.
    Now say this to him . . . 'What kind of a father do you think you were to me' – say it . . .
    Now, change places . . . be your father . . . What do you say to your son (*etc.*).

Phase 1 – Relax Physically (Variation)

Prompt Sheet 36

Make yourself comfortable – taking time out for **yourself** . . . and focus on your breathing – take two or three long, slow, deep breaths and each time – focus on the outgoing breath . . . blow it out gently by way of the mouth . . . slowly, easily . . . is the way to let go. If any thoughts intrude . . . smile and ignore them . . . you know their game . . . just let them go. Now – become aware of your legs – useful things – and stiffen the muscles in your knees – stretch . . . hold . . . relax . . . stiffen . . . relax . . . and notice how good it feels as you release any tension from your leg muscles . . . point your toes . . . and relax . . . feel the energy flow.

Now – do the same with your shoulders, arms and hands . . . tense and relax . . . tense and relax. Fan your fingers out wide . . . and let your hands relax. Stress check often, until you relearn the art of relaxing – you will respond more appropriately when a need arises . . . you will respond with SRA . . . spontaneous right action.

Now, your face and jaw muscles – grimace, stretch your jaw – mouth wide open – waggle your head . . . **relax**. Close your eyes tightly . . . open . . . now let them close gently and feel the sense of relaxation spread all the way down to your toes – and notice how good it feels. And from time to time . . . just relax . . . stretch and relax to Phase One . . . stay tuned in to yourself . . . and choose to feel good.

FOREST TRIP

Prompt Sheet 37

And now go even deeper into relaxation – deeply into the deepest realm of creative mind . . . control mind . . . the treasurehouse mind . . . and reach out to the **child**-mind within . . . see her smile as you reach out and embrace . . . you are going on a journey together . . . a journey of your choosing . . . because then . . . of course . . . all journeys are of your own choosing . . . though we sometimes forget how we make the choice . . .

And it's night-time now – a glorious night of moonlight and stars – a night made for lovers . . . a night when even the angels sigh . . . and you are deep in a mysterious forest . . . and the moonlight is shining on an ancient temple deep in the darkest part of the forest.

Great silence . . . and you enter . . . surrounded by a strange violet light that illuminates a great hall . . . and strange but kindly people appear – and they invite you to sit with them . . . and one, who is a beautiful woman with radiant green eyes . . . makes a gentle gesture with an elegant hand . . . and a glowing ball of golden light is there in front of you . . . and she smiles and explains . . . and one by one, all the people in your life who have hurt or harmed or shamed or betrayed you in any way . . . appear . . . one by one . . . and as each one appears . . . you see how you have contributed in some way or another . . . perhaps just through your presence . . . to whatever happened between you . . . in ways your conscious mind conveniently forgot . . . and will now recall . . . you will see clearly how the relationship problems arose.

In the stillness that follows . . . the person who hurt you the most will appear . . . when the person is here – your 'Yes' finger will rise.
  Is the person a man or a woman?
  Who is it? Convey your feelings . . . express them fully now . . . as you couldn't do before . . .

What do you want to do to him/her? . . .
(*Physical release*). Now . . . can you forgive . . . and forget?

Come back now and know that you can travel alone to that temple in the forest . . . to that centre of power and control in yourself – to find *your* answers to whatever *you* need to know . . . to resolve whatever problems you need to resolve . . . to become aware of all your options in life . . . to make wise choices . . . to be guided to spontaneous right action . . . every new moment of now.

You are a centre – a focal point – for vast creative expression . . .
Open to it – open to it . . . know where the power is . . . go there . . . you will be helped . . .

You will be healed . . . **right in the moment**.
Be grateful . . . be discreet . . . move on to greater things.
You will find that you do better than well – **much** better than well.

You excel.

CHANGING EMOTIONS

Prompt Sheet 38

First the event – then the emotion – then the thought – then your reaction.

Anything that stirs the same emotion can trigger the same response . . . triggered a few times . . . it establishes a trace . . . a pathway . . . a habitual pattern of response . . .

The stronger the emotion – the stronger the habit . . . and fear of rejection is a strong motivator . . . our basic need is for love, respect, support, acceptance, approval.

And we need that acceptance ourselves . . .

Accepting ourselves as we are . . . and blossoming from there. You can't blossom – striving to become – like expecting a plant to grow if you keep pulling it up to examine the roots . . . speak to the roots – yes . . . that's where the real work is done!

How are you . . . what's happening down there? Can I help in any way from here? Perhaps by just letting you **be** . . . so . . . dream for 60 seconds.

Anger: that's a secondary response . . . what feeling causes the anger . . . what caused the previous feeling?

Press your shoulders back and take a long, slow, deep breath and as you exhale . . . feel yourself relax.

You can't relax by doing something – you relax by doing nothing . . . you first do something – you tense – then relaxation can happen.

You can't change from what you know . . . you will bring what you know into the future with you. You change from what you have forgotten . . . from a state of mind beyond the beyond that you know – from long before your mother and father were born. So I don't point out a new path in life for you – I show you how to expand your options. I don't advise you to choose a lifestyle – that's your business. You're already full of advice . . . of what others think.

75

Back to childhood . . . back to those impressionable years . . . learning to adapt our feelings to our circumstances . . . forming habit patterns . . . some maladaptive feelings of low self-esteem – inability to cope, fears of rejection that stifle our ability to realise our true potential . . . I'm going to mention some feelings . . . and you will link and connect the feelings to real events in your life.

- **Jealousy** for example – feeling that you are not getting the attention you are due – and jealous of someone who seems to be getting your share . . . wanting to be the centre of attention . . . link and connect to a real event . . . your index finger will rise when you're there.
- **Anxiety** . . . anxious to make a good impression . . . worried about what people will think . . . uptight. Be there and indicate when you are.
- **Possessiveness** . . . Not sharing things . . . everything's **mine**.
- **Avoiding responsibility** . . . It wasn't my fault – it was your fault.
- Feelings of **guilt** . . . It was all my fault . . . I'm going to keep feeling bad about that.
- **Perfectionism** . . . Everything has to be my way – do it my way or it's wrong.
- **Playacting** . . . Pretending there was something wrong with you to avoid doing something.

    Link and **connect** to a time when you did that.

And know that we all do our best – at the time – the best within the bounds of your life understanding . . .

So just relax and forgive . . . live and let live . . . learning to handle our emotions . . . our relationships . . . is part of the game of life . . . you will find that you can play it . . . and win.

'Previous Life' Experiences

Prompt Sheet 39

As part of your healing process – I will ask subcon to respond with a 'Yes' or 'No' signal to the following questons . . .

- **Is any prebirth experience an important influence on xxxx's present lifestyle . . .? (*Yes*). Was it the initial sensitising event in creating his/her xxx problem?**
- **At the count of three, subcon will bring to awareness the prebirth experiences which contribute in any way to your present problems** – and we can discuss them.
- Your thumbs will waggle to indicate to me that you're learning about an important psychic event.
- What's happening . . . you can report . . . What time in your development is it . . .? at conception . . . as an embryo . . . as a foetus?
- Relax . . . and in the next thirty seconds – subcon will reveal how the experience links and connects with compounding influences and your current problems.
- Is there an earlier sensitising event – an earlier life experience?

1. Back to see the influence of earlier lifetime events on your present lifestyle.

2. Focus for a moment on a present problem area – let's see how the seeds were sown.

3. 'Conscious' life . . . green . . . **other** intervals . . . deep purple. **Electronic clock calendar** – forward or back for centuries . . . today . . . we'll choose back.

4. Stay with the feeling you want to explore.

5. Clock speeding back . . . some dates brighter . . . darker . . . experiences of joy and sadness . . . bright . . birth . . . violet . . .

purple . . . deep purple . . . dark green . . . lighter again . . . faster . . . perhaps many purple periods . . . allow subcon to choose.

6. **Back . . . back** to an experience adding purpose and depth and quality of understanding and enjoyment to your ongoing living reality . . . Back at the count of three . . . back as a witness if you choose . . . or be there seeing the event unfold . . . learning from the event that was perhaps too fleeting at the time – you are receptive at all levels now, you seek to be free from all self-limiting negative influences.

7. Electronic clock/calendar slowing down now . . . subcon is carefully choosing . . . choosing with **exquisite care** . . .

8. At the count of zero . . . you are back as a witness to a previous life experience . . . step into the time-frame, into the event at the count of zero . . . 3 . . . 2 . . . 1 . . . zero (*) . . . **get the feeling.**

9. **Look around you, child of eternity . . . there's a lesson for you to learn . . . any unfinished business – finish it with love in your heart – when you're ready to come back and report – nod your head . . . if anything disturbs you . . . your thumbs will waggle . . .**

10. Return to present time.

Slow Responses

Prompt Sheet 40

Now – we're all rather conditioned to be resistant to change . . . even though we know that change is the essence of life . . . so if you want to consider every response you make carefully with your conditioned thinking patterns – that's all right with me . . . but you'll go on your way much the same as you were when you came.

I'd prefer you to move to a more elevated vantage point in life where you can be spontaneous in your responses . . . functioning from your real centre of power . . . so that you clear all the self-limiting material and leave here a person fully responsible and in charge of yourself – capable always of spontaneous right action – awake to the wonderful options available to you in life . . . dropping the sham . . . no longer fooling yourself.

So . . . let's go to that level . . . and let's hear your responses coming **fast** and **true** . . . so . . . focus on your senses . . .

sense – that you have ten toes . . .

stretch them – let them relax . . .

and now your hands . . . stretch them – feel them relax . . .

now your jaw . . . your lips . . . become aware of the sensitivity . . . perhaps the dryness of your lips . . . and relax them into a tiny smile . . . and feel the smile spreading to your eyes . . . and focus on the sensitivity of your tongue . . . and finding excess saliva there, just swallow it . . . and go to a deeper – a more creative state of relaxation where all your responses will now be more spontaneous – more real!

Talents

Prompt Sheet 41

In whatever you choose to do in life . . . you have the capacity for excellence – everyone has – yet we can be diverted and misled . . . our inborn talents can be inhibited or repressed . . . they can be deeply buried . . . and in a moment . . . as you relax even deeper and at the count of 3 . . . you will clearly see the unique talents that you have that are seeking to find full expression in your everyday living reality . . . 1 . . . 2 . . . 3 . . . (*).

Now, these may be talents that you are presently applying to enhance your lifestyle . . . or they may be skills and talents that have been waiting to be realised – to be made real . . . whatever . . . as I touch your hand, a vivid realisation of these inborn skills and talents will come to consciousness . . . you will see and feel and know and experience that your access to this . . . to this talent . . . to this power . . . is assured . . . [*touch hand*]. Feel it, know it – experience it! You have it . . . right? Good . . . now focus on the feeling because you will go deeper now to another level of mindpower . . .
there is someone for you to meet now . . .
your own inner guide and guardian has been waiting patiently for you to transcend the limits of conditioned thought . . . in the next 30 seconds . . . you will see how you can develop for your own benefit . . . and for the benefit of all . . . be guided . . . be guided now . . . [*30 seconds*].

As you go beyond the false concepts of duality – of all those false concepts of faith and belief that give birth to doubts . . . you see the Oneness . . . the one great teacher in life . . . for you . . . is **you**.

Guilt and Shame

Prompt Sheet 42

1. *Explain timelines.*

2. Go back in your thoughts to sometime you felt very guilty . . . you felt really ashamed of yourself . . . keep the content private . . . I don't need to know anything about it . . . and you'll notice, as you focus on the event, the sense of shame or guilt is still there . . . nod when you're there.

3. Now – hop up into the timeline and move back from the event . . . go 15 minutes before it happened – see what's going on . . . nod when you're 15 minutes before it happened . . . good . . . Now . . . look forward to today . . . to now . . . and hop up into the timeline and come directly back to right now (*click fingers*) just like that . . .

4. Now . . . think of the event and try to feel guilty about it . . . try to feel guilty or ashamed about it and you'll find that you can't . . .

   How do you feel about it? Does it bother you in any way now?

We do our best at the time. From now onwards you will avoid letting your actions or reactions to any event in the past diminish your self-esteem . . . your sense of self-worth.

You will remember the process . . . you will learn from events but not let the past obscure your view of today or form a screen between you and everyday living reality.

Success

Prompt Sheet 43

1. Go to a time of success . . . don't tell me about it . . . I don't need to know what you choose . . . but be sure it was a success in which others shared in your joy . . . a success to be proud of . . . and bring on the feelings you had when you realised you had achieved something . . . it all came right more easily than you thought possible . . . nod when you've got it. (*Analyst can usually see the facial response to successful recall*).

2. Now . . . go to 15 minutes before the event and see how it happened . . . see the process unfold . . . right up to the moment you realised you had made it! OK? Now . . . double that feeling and pick a keyword that will always trigger recall of the event . . . a word or words. Got one? What is the keyword? Now – clench your fist . . . say the keyword . . . and relax. You've anchored the keyword to the feeling of success.

3. Now . . . pick an objective you have in mind . . . something you want to achieve . . . OK? Now – focus on the objective . . . say the keyword . . . tighten and release your fist.

   How does that feel? . . . good, right?

   Now, let's suppose you have an objective and you need cooperation . . . so you explain the need and you get a rejection . . . see yourself in that position . . . and what do you do? Keyword . . . fist . . . relax. Simple process, right? Very effective.

4. What does it tell you?

   In whatever you choose to do . . . you do better than well . . . **you excel** . . . see how that sounds to you . . . tell me . . . do you do better than well?

   Tell me . . . what do you do? Do you do better than well?

   Right! (*Keyword*). You will **always** excel.

82

New Skills

Prompt Sheet 44

Accept that we all have the capability of drawing on our inborn skills and talents, even if they have been inhibited or repressed . . . we can stimulate all levels of mind to respond to meet our heartfelt needs or desires.

Relax . . . and allow subcon to bring to mind someone who exhibits excellence in applying the skill or talent you seek to develop . . . someone you have seen or heard about who demonstrates mastery of the specific ability you seek to acquire.

Got someone? Good . . . now . . . focus on that person . . . it can even be someone you imagine has the capability you seek to develop.

Now . . . call on subcon to convey to you all the influences that play a part in enabling that person to perform or behave as they do. Allow subcon to bring to your awareness the pattern of stored memories . . . the actions, sounds, feelings and responses that go to provide the desirable outcome . . . relax . . . and allow the awareness to expand . . . see and hear what the other person has learned. Your index finger will rise when you have established contact or when you have received the clarification you need.

Now . . . at the count of three . . . step forward in your imagination and be that person . . . and see and feel and experience that you are actually doing what you desire to do in a masterly way . . . with all the justifiable self-confidence and competence that you need. Know and feel and experience that this capability is part of your birthright – know that the scope and power of the subconscious control mind is entirely unlimited . . . you only have to know how to convey your heartfelt needs. Subcon will ensure that the appropriate behavioural changes will be conveyed to you . . . you will be guided to SRA . . . to spontaneous right action.

Improve Performance

Prompt Sheet 45

Choose one aspect of your life or type or intensity of experience you would like to alter . . . some change you would like to experience in your lifestyle. Focus on how it is when the change has been made . . . feel the difference.

Clarify the need . . . intensify the feeling . . . send a clear picture of need to the powerhouse mind.

Now . . . in the next thirty seconds of accelerated time . . . as you relax still more deeply at the superficial levels of mind . . . subcon will allow you to re-experience with images, sounds and feelings the occasions on which you have been most effective in meeting similar needs . . . occasions when you experienced spontaneous right action . . . when what you had set out to do came right . . . and you knew it! Thirty seconds of accelerated time – starting from **now** . . . the occasions on which you succeeded just as you wanted to succeed . . . (*30 seconds*).

Now – come back to now in your thoughts – knowing that your needs have been effectively conveyed . . . knowing that whatever modifications, alterations or additions are needed to your behavioural patterns have already been initiated . . . and if others are required, you will be advised through the medium of dreams and experiences . . . you can be sure of that.

Our world is a world of words . . . watch your words.

Phase X

Prompt Sheet 46

So . . . you have experienced many phases of relaxation – you know phase five . . . when you pass through the zero to the state of conscious mind not in motion . . . you know that level and how it feels . . . so, go there now for a moment, as I ask subcon to allow you to experience phase X . . . the feeling of Oneness . . . the All-in-All . . . the transcendental state . . . at the count of three . . . to see – from that elevated viewpoint – the All-Knowing/All-Understanding state – to see the entity known as *(client)* . . . firstly . . . as a schematic – a multi-dimensional schematic of you – of the entire bodymind system – a cagework of glowing green lines . . . gently revolving . . . let's see what it reveals . . . physically first . . . in, on, around and about the schematic . . . glowing brighter whenever you focus your thoughts . . . glowing bright green . . . now watch . . .

examine the feet . . . the legs . . . the thighs . . . any red signals flashing amongst the green? Nod if there is a red signal.

Accelerated time now . . . checking for red signals . . . the stomach – reproductive organs – bladder – bowels – liver – pancreas – kidneys: all around that area – any red signals?

Now the solar plexus . . . heart . . . chest . . . lungs . . . arms . . . shoulders . . . all OK? The neck . . . the head. OK?

Now – let's review the entire system for the influences of any mental and emotional repressions . . . any maladaptive thoughts or behavioural patterns . . . switch the whole bodymind system from green to yellow . . . make it really bright and see any area signalling red . . . any part or parts, systems or functions that are inhibited in any way . . . all clear . . .? Good.

Now . . . move ten, twenty, thirty years ahead . . . review the entire bodymind system . . . how does it look? How does it feel? Good . . . that's the way you choose it to be.

So . . . thank subcon now for the experience and come on back through the phases you know – back to everyday living reality – at the count of five – back to this vibrational level of reality – **and bring the brilliance with you – bring the understanding of oneness in all things – back now to mind-in-motion . . . healing- guiding-inspiring you to more creative purpose in life . . .**

> **Awareness expanding moment to moment . . . a new quality – a new intensity of experience is now part of your lifestyle . . . feel it – know it – experience it . . . and know that you always do better than well – you excel.**

And the count is One . . . beginning to respond . . . Two . . . coming up now . . . Three . . . moving, stretching . . . Four . . . a smile on your face and a song in your heart . . . Five . . . come on back now to everyday living reality . . . and notice how good you feel.

(*If a problem area surfaces*).

All right now . . . that's good . . . focus on the signal . . . what area is signalling? Good . . . now, I'll ask subcon on your behalf to switch on any feeling associated with the problem . . . just sufficiently, subcon, to confirm that a problem exists there . . . (*click fingers*). Got the feeling? Right – now – back to the causal event . . . the initial sensitising event at the count of three . . . at the count of three, a word will spring to mind that will link and connect to the causal event . . . 1 . . . 2 . . . 3 . . . and the word is . . .??

Now – when I repeat the word . . . you'll be back in the event (*word*) . . . there you are . . . tell me what's happening – are you alone or with someone? . . . (*Have you been born?* . . . *etc.*).

Clear the problem . . . verify all systems OK . . . forward 10, 20, 30 years.

The Awakening

Prompt Sheet 47

So, little by little the clouds of illusion all clear from the inner sky and you will see what you missed or misinterpreted in life . . . and . . . more importantly – precisely how you contributed by lack of understanding, to some or all of the events that arose, if only to the extent of being in a particular place at a particular time.

So – right now – how do you choose to respond to your awakening? Do you continue to mourn over what you seemingly missed in life – or appreciate that you can benefit from the experience – and develop new skills to serve you well in the future? Your thinking is conditioned – it is a linear process – it allows you to ponder only one thing at a time . . . and whatever you repeatedly focus your thoughts on with emotion conveys as a need to the control levels of mind . . . the mental pictures you paint in consciousness serve as an attracting force – they tend to manifest – to become your own living reality.

So . . . you can live with ghosts of the past, if that is the game you choose . . . you can play childhood dependency games all your life if you fail to grow up – or you can forgive and forget and introduce a new quality of excitement and experience into your lifestyle – more poised – more self-confident, responsive and responsible – aspiring to spontaneous right action . . . developing your insight and intuition to creative purpose . . . a joy to yourself as well as to others – an inspiration . . . the choice is yours. Only your past conditioning has limited you – as the clouds clear – you can now see your options and you will be delighted to see how many options there are. In this world of duality – of two-way channels – the future you are seeking is always seeking you . . . now you know how to find it. Use the process . . . until the process is no longer required.

Just relax and go to where the stillness is. You will always do much better than well . . . you will excel! Wonderful!

Test for Suggestibility – The Elman Test

Prompt Sheet 48

Just raise your right index finger like this please (*pointing upwards*) . . . and I want you to think that, at the count of three, you will find that you won't be able to bend that finger – it will stay so rigid it won't bend . . . now watch . . . one . . . make it rigid . . . two . . . really stiff . . . three . . . so rigid you can't bend it no matter how hard you try . . . now just try to bend it and you'll find it gets stiffer and stiffer . . . it just won't bend . . . no . . . no . . . I want you to think you can't bend it . . . don't think you can bend it . . . want this to happen . . . and it happens . . . it's all as easy as that . . . just want it to happen . . . raise your finger . . . now . . . want it to happen . . . one . . . two . . . three . . . make it really rigid and now . . . find you can't bend it no matter how hard you try . . . the harder you try the stiffer it gets.

Now watch this . . . as my finger bends, your finger bends and when your finger touches your knuckle or your thumb, your eyes will close and you won't be able to open them . . . there you go . . . as your finger relaxes, you find yourself going into a very pleasant state of relaxation and you're going deeper and deeper and deeper all the time . . . every muscle in your body is relaxing and you find yourself going into a deeper – into a more creative state of relaxation all the time . . . and notice how good you feel. Now, when I click my fingers your eyes will open and you will feel better than you have felt in a long, long time . . . (*click*) . . . there you are . . . how do you feel? . . . pretty good, right?

Phobia Release (scenic route method)

Prompt Sheet 49

1. Visualising . . . 'telephone', the **word** conveys the picture.
2. Demonstrate . . . feelings induced/dispelled with suggestion . . . at the count of three.
3. Induce the anxiety . . . take it back to the first time.

The long NLP way (upgraded):

1. What resource do you need to deal with the problem . . . resource – or resources?

   Focus on feeling that you have that resource.

   Multiply the feeling of being able to cope by ten . . .

   Keyword/anchor. Add others . . . 'enhanced coping skills'.

2. Video . . . black-and-white still picture in front of you . . . float out from yourself . . . see you watching you on the TV screen.

3. Now, run a phobic scene/incident/experience/event from start to finish – see yourself responding phobically – in the grip of some unreasoned fear.

   Now . . . run the video back fast.

4. Now . . . run the video again . . . make it as real as you can . . . now run the video back to the beginning again.

5. This time . . . start the video . . . and be there in the scene . . . feel it happening to you . . . use the resource keyword . . .

   How different does it feel to you now?

6. *Analyst . . . paint a heavy scene – verify that the keyword is effective.* 'Soon . . . spontaneously cancel the maladaptive response'.

7. Verify effectiveness of the keyword at the conscious level.

Depression

Prompt Sheet 50

Having found out sometime how to induce a feeling of deep depression you have conditioned the control levels of mind to repeat it . . . you can rely on it happening now . . . it has become part of your behavioural pattern. Let's see how you started it . . . then you can substitute a more useful pattern. Depression is a learned response – it can be unlearned.

Can you forgive people for doing what they **thought** was best . . .? That's what thought does! When it's conditioned . . . and all thoughts are conditioned – even this one . . . that's the human dilemma – that's the level you can get stuck at . . . or you can choose to transcend. You can change . . . not by talking about it . . . not by thinking about it. Intellect is not the way. **Intellect has no healing power**.

You change by initiating a process of change . . .

I can convey the process . . . you can initiate it.

What was your intention . . . that's always what counts . . . not what happened.

The person who offended you . . . hurt you . . . what was their intention . . . sex abuse? Failure then to distinguish between need and greed – failure to consider the other person's right of choice . . . in this case . . . yours . . . failure to learn how to overcome their own past conditioning that has clouded their vision of what is fair and what is inexcusable. They will not be punished for their sin of ignorance – they are punished by it . . . confined to the lower mental and emotional pastures for life . . . confined by their conditioning to a level of consciousness that misses all the best options in life. Forgive them. They carry a heavier burden of self-limiting negative conditioning than you do.

Habit Change

Prompt Sheet 51

So you have a habit pattern or influence on your behaviour that you don't want – that you find is self-inhibiting ... self- limiting ... you're conscious of it ... but conscious effort to correct it has been ineffective ... so what does that tell you?

It tells you that the pattern is being controlled at a level other than the conscious one ... and as it is not happening all the time ... something is triggering the unwelcome response ... something that created the response in the first place. If we can see what that was ... then we can change the signals ... so ... let's do that ... with the help of subcon ... with the help of your powerhouse mind.

And how do you change a subconscious pattern? Not by thinking about it ... reading about it ... talking about it ... but by initiating a process of change. Initiate the process ... subcon takes over from there and does the rest ... does what your conscious levels of mind are incapable of doing.

So ... just relax ... and know that your inner-mind wants you happy, healthy ... and more and more aware of your own creative ... constructive and life-sustaining powers. It seeks to find *creative expression through you! Your purpose in life is a simple one ... your purpose in life is to enjoy.*

Reminders

Prompt Sheet 52

1. *Introducing Ideomotor Responses*

Now as I count down from eight to zero – allow yourself to drift into harmony and balance at all levels of mind . . . so that subcon can respond with finger movements to my questions . . . designed to establish the initial sensitising event that has resulted in your present-day problem – what we identify at the so-called conscious level as xxxx . . . eight . . . going deeper now . . . seven . . . more fully relaxed . . . etc. . . .

Subcon – are we at a suitable level for ideomotor responses please? (*We? Client and analyst*).

2. *Ego-State*

There seems to be a part of you that is encouraging you to act in ways that are unsuitable for your present-day needs or desires . . . and I know that it will be doing this with your best interests at heart for reasons that seem to be appropriate from where it functions.

As part of your healing process, I'd like to understand that intention – and to see if we can develop a more immediate, a more appropriate and a more life-enhancing way of meeting the needs of the entire bodymind system.

So I'd like to invite the part or parts to an informal chat – to get to know one another better – and when the part is ready to do so – I'd like it to say: 'OK (*Analyst*) – I'm ready' . . .

Thank you part . . . do you have a name please? . . .

3. *Ego-state Variation, if Response is Inadequate*

Subcon – could you advise the part responsible that it is using a reaction-pattern based on a one-time event that is now triggering a

92

series of maladaptive responses . . . it is actually creating a serious problem – which I'm sure is not the intention. To understand how to suggest a better response, I need its full cooperation and understanding . . . for the benefit of all. We need to instigate an immediate healing process . . . and I know that the part can help.

The current action is a response-pattern that has no validity today. The energies directed to it can be put to much better use.

4.   *Further Ego-state Variation*

Your head will nod in a moment when all levels of mind recognise that the strength both of your feelings and of your symptoms is a reflection of how much some deeper level of mindpower needs to be recognised and relieved right now.

Subcon – is there a level of mind or a part or parts or a system or function that is holding on to some repressed emotion . . . or is locked into responding to emotions or events in an outdated or inappropriate way?

I will refer to that out-of-phase aspect as Part X.

May I communicate with Part X either vocally or through the medium of finger signals please? Can you explain to Part X that its actions are inappropriate and outdated and provide it with three alternative options – more immediate, more appropriate and more life- enhancing processes for the benefit of the entire bodymind system – including itself please?
Has the part accepted one of the options? (etc.).
Can all levels of mind and being now cooperate fully in the healing process?
How do you feel now?

5.   *The Objective of Analysis is . . .*

. . . to show you how to take charge of your thinking processes and emotional patterns instead of allowing them to dominate you. You're being bluffed by exaggerated feelings . . . bluffed by your own thoughts.

6.   *Deepening*

Now just tell yourself in a moment as I lift your arm and let it flop back on your lap, that you'll go seven times more deeply into relaxation . . . tell yourself that and feel it happen. Notice how good it feels to get more in touch with your sensing system, less distracted by thoughts.

7.   *The Need to Prove Yourself Worthy?*

The more you develop your understanding, the less you experience the need to justify yourself to anyone – including yourself . . . you can become part of the ongoing scene without becoming contaminated by it.

8.   When I count to three and lift and drop your arm – the numbers will all be gone.

9.   Panic attack: Unreasoned fear – defenceless – heart thumping – gasping for air – feeling faint – hot and cold flushes. Autonomic nervous system out of kilter.

10. What do you need to develop – you have the potential to do anything – you have all the coping skills and more – enthusiasm, imagination, willpower, insight, flexibility, perception, sense of direction, sensitivity, humour, instinct, hope, trust-in-self, intuition, competence, precognition skills, justifiable self-confidence and courage, sincerity, tolerance, resilience, determination, honesty, love-understanding, assertiveness, depth of feeling, originality and initiative.

11. Ideodynamics . . . establish age and pinpoint the event . . . then at the count of zero you will go back to the event (or 15 minutes before) and you'll be able to tell me what's happening to you . . . and around you.

As I count backwards from eight to zero – feel yourself getting smaller and smaller – younger and younger – until you're back at the event or experience . . . to the initial sensitising event . . . only this time . . . to fifteen minutes before and you will see the event unfold. (*Or to the event in which the word xxxx has significance*). Reinforce ideomotor responses if there is no clear response:

Now, I'm putting this index finger under the direct control of your inner mind . . . so let it get stiffer . . . stiffer – that's right . . . and now try to raise it and you'll find that it just won't move . . . it gets stiffer the more you try to raise it. Good.

Now, try to raise it consciously and you'll find that it remains exactly where it is. Good. Now, subcon . . . please move the finger to signify '**yes**'. Thank you, subcon.

Alternatively:

I'm going to put your fingers under the control of your subconscious control mind so that we can get the information we need to harmonise all levels of mind and resolve the problems that have been troubling you. You'll find that this index finger will rise to respond '**yes**' to questions and this finger will rise to signify '**no**' . . . and if there is any conscious mind interference, your thumbs will waggle . . . and I'll ask subcon now if this signalling system is acceptable please. (*There is no need to check the negative or you can check the negative by asking 'Is there any objection to me acting as part of xxxx's healing system for the benefit of the entire bodymind system?'*).

12. Avoid 'why's' . . . 'Your Dad didn't love you . . . because? Finish the sentence.

'Because your mother no longer treated him as the only person she loved' . . . is that what happened? Put your Dad over there and ask him . . .

13. *Jealousy – suggestions for behavioural change*

'What can I do to show her how much I love her?'

'What can I do today to show her that I'm worthy of her trust and love?'

14. The need to convert others to your beliefs and opinions is a neurotic compulsion – it can be treated.

15. Now close your eyes as you start to direct more of your attention inwards.

Give yourself five minutes a day just sitting, within a week you can relax creatively anywhere, relaxing that way you get any emotional log-jam loosened up nicely.

16. What triggers the negative response? Anchor a spontaneous positive response to it . . . you get more spontaneous the more you practise.

17. Establish what is the first awareness that a phobic response is developing . . . is it a person, place, voice, look, feeling, taste, sound, smell or sight?

18. *Test for relaxation at the basement level* – try to lift a leg . . . try to open eyes . . . *any movement, go to the sub-basement . . . through the zero, if necessary. Bring to a 'tuned-in' level* – 'tuned inwards to subcon you will now find you can move to a more elevated – to a more creative level of mind . . . at the count of three . . . 1 . . . 2 . . . 3 . . .' (*).

19. Each and every beneficial suggestion will bring about the desired changes within the next seven days – you will experience a

gradual release of tension as the repressed emotions of the past are allowed to vent.

20. Things we do – to get attention – often become habitual behavioural patterns – smoking, drinking etc.

21. Let's see if the next time has the same elements – repetition making it habitual . . . a conditioned reflex. When I click my fingers . . . it will be the next time . . . you'll be there . . . (*) . . . . there you are. We'll find the same elements in the most recent occurrence – basically – the need for comfort – security – now . . . watch (*) . . . there you are . . . it's the most recent time.

22. Now you can relax to a certain degree but creative relaxation is something you need to be guided to do . . . when you reach that elevated state . . . you'll know it and I will . . . and what's more important – you will always retain the knack.

23. And you'll be surprised to find just how easy it is to let go . . . each breath taking you to deeper levels of awareness . . . so that things that have relevance to your health and enjoyment in life that you think you have forgotten will surface and all self- limiting negativity will be released from your bodymind system for ever.

24. Let's see that awareness increase as you go back in your thoughts to a holiday time . . . a happy holiday time – nod when you have the feeling. Now take that feeling all the way back through the years to the very first time you went to the seaside . . . be there at the count of three . . . 1 . . . 2 . . . 3 . . . (*).

And now your first day at school . . .

You see, there's a vast treasurehouse of self-understanding available to you . . . you will see how we develop habitual thinking patterns that influence our wellbeing and our general enjoyment of life.

25. *Repressions.* Whenever you push something out of your awareness . . . you give it strength . . . the longer you do that . . . the more strength you feed it . . . it can overwhelm you . . . it's like holding a beach-ball under water. Stop pushing . . . stop resisting . . . just relax and let it pop into consciousness . . . you release the energy for more creative purpose.

26. *Loneliness.* So you're lonely. First of all . . . you learned how to ignore your own love . . . your own understanding of your own natural needs. You either concentrated on other things or you pre-

ferred to live in illusion . . . you alienated yourself from other people – now you call it 'loneliness' . . . so let's see how the loneliness pattern . . . the alienation pattern . . . started.

I'll ask subcon to let you experience exactly where that feeling of loneliness is in the body . . . at the count of three . . . 1 . . . 2 . . . 3 . . . where do you feel it?

Now . . . to make sure that that is where the physical feeling emanates from . . . when I snap my fingers . . . subcon will bring the feeling on more strongly . . . (*). Now . . . as I count down from six to zero . . . subcon will take you back in time to the very first time that something or somebody triggered the emotional and physical response . . . six . . . getting younger and younger . . . five . . . your legs and arms are growing shorter and shorter . . . four . . . etc.

27. *Perfection* – is not a human attribute. Say this . . . 'I have to be perfect because then people will admire me.' Fine – now finish this sentence . . . 'I have to be perfect because . . .' 'Because I don't like to be criticised.' And again 'I have to be perfect because . . .' 'Because my dad will be angry.'

So – let's go back to the first time you learned that you had to live up to someone else's expectations . . . I'll touch your forehead and you will know who wanted you to be something they wanted you to be.

28. *'CLICK' focuses awareness . . . momentarily. Don't always click fingers . . . touch forehead . . . hand . . . raise or lower the arm.*

29. What's happening now? Not . . . 'What's causing that?'

'Doesn't feel right'. That's what it doesn't do . . . how **does** it feel? Where do you feel it?

Just relax and . . . for the next sixty seconds . . . let thoughts come to mind that have relevance to your problem . . . to the cause or causes of your problem. (*It's a good way of giving yourself time, with the help of subcon, to figure where you're going next . . . go to your fingers – and relax*).

A spontaneous remission is the result of a dramatic shift in awareness. It can be initiated.

A physical wound . . . there's a mental and emotional wound too . . . and vice versa.

Highly-stressed people are suffering from the disease of being in a hurry.

Old people . . . from *psychosclerosis* – hardening of the attitudes. The only difference between people is a question of consciousness – their degree of consciousness. The game controls the game-player . . . you can still be helped . . . if helping is someone else's game. Analysis is a game that two can play.

30. Listen to the predicates in a person's speech . . . seeing . . . hearing . . . feeling . . . smelling . . . tasting. This can sometimes help you.

31. Induce deep relaxation – stretch arm . . . tell the person to open eyes . . . to see their arm *is* stuck out there, no longer under their conscious control. Handy for people who doubt the power of suggestion.

32. If there were only **one** thing you could improve in your lifestyle today – what would you choose to improve . . . let's make your need really specific. And now . . . another . . . and later, we will ask subcon to bring to mind any other points that need to be cleared while we are here together.

33. You can notice how your awareness is increasing – increasing, in fact, with every breath that you take – and this two-way communication channel will always be open to you in the future whenever you need it . . . you will respond to any situation that arises with spontaneous right action.

Critical Faculty Bypass (Optional Test)

Prompt Sheet 53

What is your telephone number?

Wouldn't it be interesting to find that you can visualise your telephone number as though it is written on the telephone at home and you can choose to erase the number from your memory for sixty seconds so that, no matter how hard you try, you can't see or say the number?

When you can erase it that way . . . and you can . . . you know that any time you want you can relax your mind, because you can choose precisely what you want to think about and what you want to ignore.

Now . . . as I raise and drop your hand the telephone number will drop from your thoughts and when you are sure you have a relaxed mind – open your eyes.

Fine . . . now . . . try to tell me your telephone number and you'll find it is gone . . . gone completely . . . try really hard . . .

You see, if you really want to take charge of your conditioned mind, you can do it . . . then you are in control of it . . . and not the other way around! Just tell it to relax . . . do you want that to happen? Good . . . so close your eyes and relax them to the point where they just won't work and when you are sure that they won't work . . . test them and make sure they are relaxed. As I count from three to zero, relax all other numbers away for a minute – 3 . . . 2 . . . 1 . . . (*click*) . . . now open your eyes and try really hard to remember your telephone number. And now relax . . . at the count of three, the number becomes clear to you . . . 1 . . . 2 . . . 3. What's your telephone number?

In future, when you or I say 'Phase Two relaxation', you will relax your conditioned mind and yet be more aware . . . more in control at all levels of mind.

99

Seal-Breaking, Elman Style

Prompt Sheet 54

Raise an index finger as you say to the client: point an index finger towards the ceiling and I want you to think that when I count to three you will not be able to bend that finger no matter how hard you try to bend it . . . it will stay completely rigid. Now watch (one) make it rigid . . . (two) . . . absolutely rigid . . . (three) . . . you make it so rigid that it just won't bend no matter how hard you try . . . in fact, it gets more and more rigid . . .

(No . . . no . . . I want to show you how to take charge of your thoughts . . . I want you to *think* that you *can't* bend it . . . *want* this to happen . . . don't want it not to happen . . . if you want it to happen, it happens. This time, really *want* it to happen).

Stiffen your finger . . . and want it to stiffen one . . . two . . . three . . . (*click*) . . . now you find it gets stiffer the more you try to bend it . . . the harder you try to bend it . . . the stiffer it gets . . . good . . . now watch this.

As my finger bends, your finger bends and as it bends, your eyes start to close – as my finger bends – your finger bends and now that your eyes are closing you can bend your finger as your eyes gently close and you find yourself drifting into a light level of relaxation – as your eyes close you drift still deeper . . . *very* relaxed, drifting into a more creative state of physical and mental relaxation than you have perhaps known for years . . . relaxed, but with increased awareness – in fact, as you allow yourself to drift deeper and deeper your awareness is increasing by more than three thousand percent and you can go to any significant event in your life and be there again – right in the moment.

All conscious self-hypnosis seals are gone completely . . . you can relax physically and mentally in future when it is appropriate simply by saying 'Phase Two relaxation'.

An alternative seal-breaking theme used by Dave Elman:

Somebody talked to you in the past about hypnosis . . . can you picture that person? Perhaps you can visualise better with your eyes closed. Do you remember him saying something like – when you close your eyes they won't open? (*Yes*). So just test them and make sure they won't open.

Instant Pain Relief

Prompt Sheet 55

This simple process has proved effective in dealing with intractable pain by telephone, speaking directly to the sufferer or to a companion who need have no understanding of the process.

The reason for its effectiveness is simply that a person suffering in this way is already in an altered state of consciousness and can respond spontaneously to beneficial suggestions.

> 'Close your eyes and pretend that you can't open them no matter how hard you try and the pain won't bother you half as much. Now – open and close your eyes twice and the pain will be nearly all gone. Now – open your eyes and inhale deeply – exhale . . . and let go all the pain . . . all the pain is now gone.'

('You lost that relaxation – open and close your eyes . . . exhale . . . and all the pain is gone').

> 'Now mentally repeat . . . one, two, three relax . . . relax . . . and notice how good you feel . . .'

Contrary to the experience of many other therapists, I find that a pain can be called a pain. Referring to a pain as 'discomfort', for example, could convey to the sufferer that you have failed to appreciate the full extent of his need.

Body Image

Prompt Sheet 56

Nice and easy now . . . see yourself standing in front of you . . . see yourself exactly as you choose to be . . . exactly as you want to be . . . and know that you have the potential to be . . . cancel any thoughts that limit your potential and be what you choose to be . . . put your ideal body image there in front of you . . . when you have it clearly in mind, your right index finger will rise.

Now make it even more real . . . and see yourself step forward and fit snugly into that ideal body shape . . . make sure it's exactly what you want – make any adjustments you like – it's your choice . . . always your choice . . . move around in it . . . enjoy it . . . feel the strength and energy and beauty in it . . . and know that you are conveying a clear picture of your needs to your powerhouse mind . . . and your needs will be met. At the count of three, the precise shape, form, weight and condition will be there – clearly in your mind . . . 1 . . . 2 . . . 3 . . . (*).

The image of your ideal body shape and condition is now conveyed and will serve as a pattern – as an attracting force – your physique will be automatically adjusted to the new mould and you will become aware, day by day, of the changes in habits and behavioural patterns you will be guided to make . . . to attain . . . and maintain your ideal bodymind shape, size, form, weight and condition . . . swiftly . . . effortlessly . . . completely.

And relax . . . the message has been conveyed to control . . . just release . . . relax . . . and enjoy.

So how was your original bodymind system created? An image was created by thought . . . now you are thinking . . . again!

103

Getting Problems in Hand

Prompt Sheet 57

Just relax for a moment with your eyes closed as you bring to mind a problem you have . . . any problem at all, or allow subcon to remind you of one, if this will be beneficial to you, one that, perhaps, has not cleared from all levels of consciousness.

As the problem comes to mind, take conscious control, for a moment, of two or three deep breaths . . . focusing on prolonging the outgoing breath and feeling the sense of relaxation spreading to every nerve and cell and system of the body.

Now . . . open your eyes and raise your right hand in front of your face so that you can examine the palm of your hand and lock the fingers tightly together as you stiffen the hand and focus your eyes on the palm and notice the sensations as you allow your eyes to close while you still focus your thoughts on your hand and you will notice that the fingers naturally seek to relax and spread apart without you consciously seeking to spread them apart and as they do, you automatically become more and more relaxed . . . more aware of your gentle breathing rhythm – and as your fingers spread gently apart and the cause of your problem comes strongly to mind as your hand moves all by itself towards your face and the moment your hand touches your face the solution to the problem will spring to mind, the moment your hand touches your face and not a moment before and as you focus on the darkness that is light not yet in motion you experience a sense of expanding awareness as wider aspects of the problem present themselves to you in the mirror of your mind and as soon as the solution is ready to come clearly to mind and not a moment before, your hand will touch your face and the solution will be conveyed to you . . . brightly illuminated . . . clearly defined . . . and your hand will return to rest comfortably on your lap . . . you will be deeply refreshed – deeply relaxed – with deeper self-understanding as you return once more to everyday awakening consciousness.

104

You will practise this awareness exercise whenever it is beneficial and appropriate to do so and day by day through the medium of dreams and everyday experiences you will find yourself released from all self-limiting negativity and problems of the past . . . and they will be released from you.

At the count of five you will return to everyday living reality and notice how good you feel.

Back to the Future

Prompt Sheet 58

Just as all of us have experiences in the past that have been repressed from memory but which are accessible from a more elevated mental vantage point . . . the same level of mind is fully aware of all your inborn resources and your potential . . . your options in life can be made clearer to you. In a moment, as you continue to relax creatively, I'm going to ask subcon to bring to mind an option that you may or may not have been consciously aware of . . . your best option, taking into account your social and professional skills, your needs and desires, your health and wellbeing and any and all other facets of the good life that subcon is always fully aware of . . . to clarify for you, not necessarily for discussion unless this is also beneficial to you . . . what is your best option in life and to do so in accelerated time . . . within the next sixty seconds or so of clocktime, starting from the count of three please subcon . . . and you will signal by raising the index finger on your left or right hand when the option has been clearly conveyed . . . at the count of three subcon . . . your best option in life . . . 1 . . . 2 . . . 3 . . . (*). **Nil response** . . .

'Subcon, is there a level of mind blocking access to present and future options . . . please respond by causing this finger to rise to signify 'yes' . . . or this little finger to signify 'no'.

Thank you subcon' . . . and proceed by asking to establish communication with the level involved or request clarification of options through the medium of dreams and experiences over the next several days.

(*You may require to imagine a 'yes' or 'no' response before helping the client to achieve a more creative level of relaxation*).

Great . . . I see you have an option in mind . . . do you need to clarify it more at the moment?

Now . . . as I reach forward and touch you gently on the forehead . . . I would like subcon to move you forward five years in calendar

106

time so that you can review the influence on your lifestyle of putting your best options into play . . .

. . . the effect on your relationships and your general good health and wellbeing. Subcon will bring three major beneficial influences to mind . . . your head nodding each time so that I may keep pace with your progress . . . (*touch forehead*). Great . . . now, if there is anything else that subcon wants to convey to you . . . I will be silent for the next 30 seconds of clocktime.

Fine . . . and know that this two-way channel is always open to you . . . a creative channel . . . and you will know the answers are right . . . you know the feeling . . . you feel it in your head, your heart and your stomach . . . it is part of your being.

Thank subcon warmly with me, and bring all that is beneficial to you back to today . . . to this ever-new moment of now . . . you will remember to go there often, to clarify your options . . . and your choices will always be right . . . right for you . . . right for others . . . as long as your purpose is right.

Previous Life Experiences (2)

Prompt Sheet 59

Now, as subcon allows you to drift back in thought – drifting back through the years – through many decades, through many centuries perhaps to a time, to a date, a place, an event or an experience in your past as an egg-cell or as an entity in whatever form, for your choice as an energy form . . . as a tiny speck of stardust in eternity – as a child of the universe – is unlimited, for you are part of the eternal creative space between two thoughts, no more, no less – part of the oneness in all things, of the All-in-All – always experiencing **self** as the centre, because, of course, we are all the centre of our universe, all part of the creative void. Drifting back in terms of time now to trace the experiences that contributed to your sensitivies . . . that have been seeded in the psyche and have contributed to the illusion of limited resources: seed-mind . . . subcon choosing again with exquisite care a time, a place, an experience as a seed cell or as a persona, as an entity – going back five full lifetimes to the time, the place and the circumstances – to see and hear and feel and re-experience a significant event – you will be there at the count of four . . . knowing your age, your sex . . . you will hear your name called . . . 1 2 3 4 (*click*).

Look around you now . . . be there . . . and learn . . . there is a lesson for you to learn. (*Be prepared to reduce discomfort or emotion to half . . . and half again if necessary, by a click of the fingers*).

Now forward to how you dropped the persona . . . and now you choose again . . .

Your next living experience at the vibrational level of reality . . . come forward to the next lifetime . . . to a significant event, allow subcon to choose . . . a time, a place, an experience that had a sensitising effect . . . 1 2 3 4 (*click*) there you are, in the experience . . . seeing, hearing, feeling again . . . subcon will clarify the picture . . . will reveal the lesson. As a child of eternity, you are the student, you are the teacher . . . you are the school.

See the lesson . . . and drop that persona as you come forward in time again to your next choice, to your next living experience . . . be there at the count of four . . . 1 2 3 4 (*click*).

And now . . . to your next entry to the vibrational levels of reality and see how a significant event links to an earlier experience as an egg-cell or as an entity. Now . . . to the next adventure.

And now, coming forward in time to a significant experience in your present lifetime and see how the patterns were formed.

And now . . . release all that is unwanted, all that is unnecessarily limiting, restrictive or maladaptive and bring forward to now all that is beneficial and life-enhancing . . . and know and feel and experience your unlimited positive potential for excellence in all things.

(OPTIONAL EXTRA):

And forward now to the time you choose to drop your present persona . . . the present you gave yourself . . . choose now and be generous, knowing that you can change the date at will . . . your choice is limited only by your level of life-understanding and your understanding increases every new moment of now. Choose a date, a time . . . and choose to live with excellence to that time . . . for now you know who chooses it . . . there is only one to choose . . . so, be generous . . . and resolve – resolve to live and love and laugh and learn . . . and leave, in due time . . . resolve to leave with dignity, an inspiration to your **self**, an inspiration to your loved ones, an inspiration to everyone. And smile . . . smile . . . for now you know the gameplayer, you know who invented the game, the game you knew you can choose to win. Win it . . . win it . . . win it every day . . . now you know the way.

Representative Case History Using Precision Techniques

The following is a verbatim extract from a one-session case, the session running for less than two hours. The PS numbers are provided to identify the prompt sheets that were used. With experience, the number of prompt sheets required can be reduced to two, a session summary sheet and a copy of the closing summary. A brief information sheet is also prepared, recording the client's first name, the date and whatever needs are expressed before the session. These consciously-expressed needs will be dealt with together with the major problems that the more knowledgeable levels of mind disclose while the client is creatively relaxed.

The executive part of the therapy session usually starts with introducing the client to three levels of relaxation . . . the physical relaxation state and then the mental and creative states of relaxation, more or less as detailed in PS 9/1. In the creative state, the client usually moves to a good working level spontaneously.

The client in this case is Joan, a young woman of twenty-three. Her presenting problem was spinal cancer. She felt that she had benefited from using the Cancel Cancer I tape for a month and this was confirmed by a Lüscher test, showing a reduction in stress level from four to two. The light level of stress was further confirmed by using biofeedback. Her blood temperature and blood pressure were both slightly below the generally accepted norm. Joan agreed to the session being recorded and she easily relaxed to a good working level in less than ten minutes.

D In a moment, Joan, you will feel me touching the back of your right hand and the moment I do . . . a word will spring to mind . . . and the word will link and connect to the precise cause of your cancer problem . . . subcon will provide a two- way channel to the initial sensitising event . . . going back now . . . going back through the years and now . . . I touch your hand . . . what's the word, Joan . . . what's the word that springs to mind . . .?

J Babes (*indistinct*).

D Clearer Joan . . . what's the word . . .? Baby?

J No – 'babies'. I don't know why it's 'babies'.

D That's fine . . . 'babies' . . . just relax still more deeply as I ask subcon to bring on the feelings attached to the word 'babies'. Watch very carefully . . . at the count of three . . . the feeling will be there . . . 1 . . . 2 . . . 3 . . . (*) (click fingers) . . . there it is . . . what do you feel . . .?

J (*Head twists*) . . . It's my neck . . . my neck hurts . . .

D Fine . . . but now reduce that feeling to half (*) . . . and focus on the area . . .

J It's going down my back . . . (*twists*).

D All right, subcon, reduce the feeling (*) . . . and now I'll ask subcon to take you right back . . . with the usual provisos . . . to when that feeling first came . . . right back as I count down from three to zero . . . 3 . . . 2 . . . 1 . . . zero (*) . . . there you are . . . are you indoors or outdoors . . .?

J Indoors.

D Night or day?

J I don't know.

D You just think you don't know . . . your subcon knows. Have you been born yet?

J Yes.

D Alone or with someone?

113

J With . . . **some** . . . one (*doubtful*).

D Look very closely now . . . tell me what's happening . . . who's with you?

J It's my brother!

D . . . and what's happening?

J We're watching TV.

D Watching TV . . . what age are you?

J I'm . . . five.

D And what's on TV . . .? (*no response*) . . . Clarify the picture . . . watch it rolling now . . . 1 . . . 2 . . . 3 . . . (*) . . . there it is . . . what are you watching?

J Children's TV (*grimaces*).

D Something's disturbing you . . . what are you watching?

J Blue Peter (*very quiet*).

D Blue Peter? . . . That's a nice little programme, isn't it?

J Yes (*twisting*).

D You have this discomfort . . . is it something you see? . . . something being said?

J Something being said.

D Your brother said . . . or said on TV?

J Said on TV.

D As I pick up and drop your arm back on your lap . . . you will hear what is being said . . . there you are . . . what's being said . . .? (*Emotion . . . sobbing*). That's right . . . let it come . . . let it vent . . . it has been stuck down there for far too long . . .

J They're . . . launching an appeal . . . about something.

D . . . and the appeal is for what? Do you know what an appeal is?

J Yes . . . it's about stuff for babies when they're born . . . for premature babies . . . incubators.

D And it disturbs you?

J Yes . . . the babies are hurting . . . their heads are too big . . .

D All right now . . . just take that feeling away . . . it has no relevance to now . . . you know that incubators are to help the babies . . . and the appeal was directed to adults . . . to get their help and support. You fully understand that now. Can you let the fright go?

J Yes . . . it happened a long time ago . . .

D Good . . . now I'm going to ask subcon to establish a signalling system . . . there is information we need to exchange. So I'll ask subcon to raise this index finger when the answer to my question is 'Yes' . . . this little finger to rise to indicate 'No'.

And I want you to know that these fingers are now responding only to your subconscious control mind as we are working together . . . you and I . . . so . . . try to raise this index finger

consciously and you will find it stays still . . . try really hard . . .
now relax even deeper . . . and now I'll ask subcon if this signalling system is acceptable please so that I can help Joan for the
benefit of her entire bodymind system. (*Flickering finger signal,
right index*). Thank you subcon . . . the answer, as you know Joan,
is 'Yes' . . . and if anything disturbs you Joan, subcon will signal
to me by waggling your thumbs. So I'll ask subcon . . . subcon,
was the television appeal programme the initial cause of Joan's
spinal problem? Thank you subcon . . . the answer is 'No'. Was it
a compounding event? And the answer is 'Yes'. So we're going
further back, with the help of subcon, in a different kind of way.
Now, when we come into this life cycle or even before . . . all
levels of mind are open to receive perhaps millions of signals
about events and experiences that are going on in, on and all
around us . . . as we evolve to become part of this everyday living
reality . . . and every event is accurately recorded by subcon in
infinite detail. These events, in turn, can influence our reactions
to things that are happening today. We can accept beliefs –
herdmind concepts – without seeking for truth in ourselves – we
can be led and misled. So – when did this happen, if it did . . . if
our problems are all seeded in us at an early age . . . exactly when
did it happen . . . and how do we correct any self-limiting negative conditioning we have absorbed . . . how do we reclaim our
birthright – to enjoy a happy, healthy and fulfilling lifestyle? The
good news is that, seeing how these negatives were seeded . . .
you're going to find that they lose their inhibitory powers . . . they
will cease diverting your energies from creative purpose in life.
Now, in a moment, you're going to hear a sound – a recorded
sound – that will take you back in your thoughts to a time before
you were born . . . the nearby sound of a human heartbeat . . . a
sound that was part of your awareness month after month . . . the
sound of your mother's heartbeat. You're back in your mother's
womb . . . comforted, supported, nourished and sustained . . .
afloat in a liquid environment . . . but aware . . . (PS 7). (*Small
movements*). How was the trip into life . . . did you feel any
discomfort?

J No . . .
D But your thumb is waggling. Let me just move this arm – ah! . . .
   you've lost that relaxation . . . breathe deeply . . . now slowly
   exhale . . . and go ten times deeper into relaxation. Now as I lift
   and drop your arm, feel the difference . . . beautifully relaxed.
   Now . . . on the count of three . . . you're just being born . . . 1 . . .
   2 . . . 3 . . . (*) . . . your head's moving . . . your shoulders are

moving . . . what's happening?

J   Some silly bugger is pushing me around! (*Back arches, head presses back*). Stork.

D   Stork?

J   Stork in the tombs.

D   Stork in the . . .?

J   Stuck in the T-U-B-E-S!

D   Oh, sorry! Stuck on the way into life . . . here's the hand that is pushing you around (*pushed her wrist gently*) . . . what do you want to convey to that person . . .?

J   Get away! Leave me alone! You're making it worse! **Now I'm stuck!** (*Pushing strongly against my hand, crying*).

D   Great . . . great . . . push it away . . . you can release it now . . . it has no relevance now – that feeling has been stuck down there far too long! Is it all gone now?

J   Yes . . . it's gone . . .

D   Who was doing the pushing?

J   The doctor.

D   He was doing his best to help you . . . we always do our best . . . can you forgive him . . . not necessarily excuse him . . . but can you forgive him?

J   Yes . . . he didn't know.

D   How do you feel now . . .?

J   Very relaxed.

D   Good . . . come forward now . . . come forward half-an-hour . . . it's now half-an-hour after your birth – you've arrived – everything's fine now . . . you won your way into life against the most incredible odds and that creative spirit is still a fundamental part of you now . . . it is your own subconscious control mind.
    Let's ask subcon . . . is that the initial sensitising event subcon? The answer is 'No' . . .
    Is there an earlier event subcon? There is . . . the answer is 'Yes'. Your shoulders are still hunched . . . what's the feeling now?

J   Being hurt . . . I'm frightened of being hurt.

D   Focus on the feeling for a moment . . . as subcon takes you back – back to the womb – back before you were born . . . at the count of three . . . back you go . . . 1 . . . 2 . . . 3 . . . (*) the same feeling . . . tell me – what's happening?

J   I don't know.

D   When I lift your hand . . .

J   Mummy's fallen . . .

D   Mummy's fallen . . . you're a foetus or an embryo . . . how many months old are you . . . more than one month old?

J   Four months.
D   You're not apart from your mother . . . you are a part of your mother . . . you know how she feels . . . how does she feel?
J   She's hurt. She's very frightened. She thinks she has hurt me. She's trembling.
D   Subcon . . . did the mother's fall damage the embryo physically? The answer is 'No'.
     How was your mother hurt? You'll know when I touch your hand.
J   She has hurt her back. The chair broke.
D   Cancel the discomfort – cancel the emotion – just relax. Is this something you have been aware of consciously, Joan?
J   No . . . but I could see the broken chair. A kitchen chair.
D   Subcon . . . was this the initial causal event for the symptom we recognise as spinal cancer? Thank you subcon . . . the answer is 'Yes'.
     Now . . . link and connect the events and the feelings . . . the fall . . . being manipulated at birth . . . then the next one . . . what was the next one?
J   Watching TV.
D   Right . . . see the connection . . . the same elements . . . fear . . . trembling . . . discomfort . . . and come forward now . . . forward in time to some event with a similar emotional content . . . just before you were diagnosed as having cancer . . .
J   Oh I know what that is! Dad has died. Mother has gone to pieces . . . she always does. She's afraid of everything, even sex. She's left me with Dad. She won't stay in the house with him. She's gone next door until my brother comes.
D   How old are you?
J   I'm nineteen.
D   And how do you feel?
J   Frightened . . . trapped . . . I'm alone.
D   All right . . . but let's see if there is more to it than that. When I touch your forehead, subcon will spell out a word that will explain exactly what that feeling is, so we can all understand.
J   'B' (five more taps)R,E.E.C.H.
D   What's the word?
J   'Breech' . . . I don't know why . . . I wasn't a breech birth! I see it! I see it now . . . the feeling is that there's a gap . . . a gap in my defences . . . I'm easily frightened . . . I allow myself to be pushed around . . . dumped on. Mother still does it to me today.
D   And when you're dumped on, what's the feeling?
J   I'm being held down . . . with other people's problems.

D Where do you feel the pressure?

J My shoulders! My back! My mother has a stooped back too.

D Who has she been carrying?

J Her fears! Oh God – how stupid!

D Not really. Now you know better than most that we are locked into responding to our conditioning until we grow wiser. Just as we learn from infancy how to relate to those around us, it seems that we must learn from someone how to discover the truth in ourselves. There's a process. It has to be demonstrated. Thinking about it, talking about it, reading about it . . . moaning about it . . . is useless. We are still functioning from the conditioned levels of mind. We see through a fog of past conditioning. Now the fog is starting to shift. We each have the power to shift it . . . to understand. When it shifts, we see other options and we are guided to choose . . . we are guided to spontaneous right action!
How does your back feel now?

J Like a weight – has gone.

D . . . has been lifted off, right?

J Feels good. Why isn't life easier?

D Life is easy. Simple. We complicate it. We start by mixing up wants and needs. It becomes a game with infinite possibilities. A fun game if we learn how to play it right . . . and that's what you're about to do . . . to learn to play **your** game. The truth in you is what sets you free. Let's find some more of it. Go to phase three and notice how good you feel. Now, let's do one that is on the tape . . . let's get you more in touch with your senses . . . with your sensing system. Just become aware of your toes . . . in your stockings . . . in your shoes . . . resting on the chair. Now shift your awareness to your hands . . . to the fingers on your right hand, to the index finger . . . to the little finger . . . good. Now to your lips . . . and now raise the corners of your lips in a tiny smile . . . because relaxation is a pleasant experience . . . something to enjoy several times a day at least until relaxing creatively becomes a habit, a spontaneous response. And now focus your awareness on your tongue . . . still maintaining the smile . . . and as excess saliva begins to form in your mouth . . . just swallow it . . . and go down, down, down – still deeper into relaxation.
Now reach up in your imagination and bring the mental sunshine down and into the body by way of the head and focus it now on any area of discomfort or concern in the body . . . and see if there is any area that seems to be vibrating at a different rate from the tissue around it . . . this will reflect as a different tone or colour . . . what can you see? Shine the light around, see what you can see.

J   It's darker . . . purple . . . dark purple.
D   What shape is the dark area? Is it like anything you know?
J   It's like a little pear!! A tiny pear! It has spots on it – white spots.
D   How big is it . . . an inch long . . . half an inch long?
J   About a centimetre . . . it's very small.
D   Now . . . leave the light there. I'm going to move you forward three months from now . . . the light knows what to do, the bodymind system knows how to respond. At the count of three, it will be the fifteenth of January 1989 – move three months ahead . . . 1 . . . 2 . . . 3 . . . and now . . . follow the light down . . . how does that area look now?
J   It's . . . shiny . . . nice and shiny. Just a tiny dark speck . . . almost gone.
D   Now move another three months ahead, to the fifteenth of April . . . how does it look now?
J   Completely . . . completely better!
D   That picture has been conveyed to all levels of mind . . . it is now your living reality. Is that correct, subcon? (*index finger signals 'Yes'*). There you are . . . you have your answer . . . the answer is 'Yes'. Mentally thank subcon . . . as I do too.

We are not empowered to create lifeforce. We are not empowered to destroy it. It seems that we are empowered to direct it, to focus it . . . which we can do with understanding, or even with lack of it! Through lack of understanding, we can be clumsy with the controls. You will find that your ability to direct your powers to healthy, creative, life-sustaining purpose will continue to increase day by day. Your powers will reflect in your behaviour.

Allow this to inspire others and be discreet in your choice of words. An important concept, worth considering, is expressed in the Cancel Cancer II tape . . . there is no malignancy in Nature. 'Malignancy' is an error of thought, of the conditioned, thinking levels of mind, born through lack of self-understanding.

So . . . let's ask the source of truth in you . . . subcon . . . is it correct that the tumour-forming cells in Joan's bodymind system have been forming what we recognise as a tumour as a form of self-protection? . . . As you are aware, Joan, the answer is 'Yes'. Thank you, subcon. Can whatever signals that initiated this tumour-forming action be corrected now, please? (*Yes*).

May I communicate in words to all cells and functions involved in defending themselves and in attacking? (*Yes*).

Are all cells receptive to my words, subcon? (*Yes*).

Thank you, subcon . . . I'm speaking as part of Joan's healing process to all cells and functions involved, directly or indirectly,

in tumour-forming or in attacking the tumour-forming cells . . .
please, immediately cease these activities and return immediately to normal healthy functioning. An error in communication of
needs or some other process has occurred which subcon will now
proceed to correct by instituting a more immediate, a more appropriate and a more life-sustaining process at the count of three.
Subcon, is this acceptable at all levels? (*Signal . . . 'Yes'*). 1 . . . 2 . . .
3 . . . (*). Thank you subcon. Are all parts and functions of the
bodymind system responding and benefiting, subcon? (*Signal . . .
'Yes'*).
Are there any major problems that can be dealt with right now,
subcon? (*'No' . . . uncertain finger movement*). Thank you, subcon
. . . I got the message.
Now, Joan . . . go still deeper . . . deep, deep down . . . phase four,
sub-basement . . . notice how deeply you can go now all by
yourself . . . and subcon will ensure that you only use these levels
when it is appropriate for your own health and wellbeing to do
so.
You have the same powers of mind that anyone . . . **anyone** ever
born to this planet has ever had . . . to this extent, we are all born
equal. Nature doesn't play favourites. Nature seeks to find expression for creative purpose in trillions of ways . . . and you are
one of them . . . and this is a simple exercise. I want you to go back
to the very, very first time you walked . . . instead of crawling
around the floor, seeing tables from underneath, seeing only
what you could see from near the ground floor level . . . accepting
it, because, at that stage, that was all you felt you could do . . . and
suddenly you found you could stand and your whole perspective
changed . . . go back to that first time . . . the first time you walked
. . . and tell me . . . where are you . . . indoors or outdoors?
J I'm in the kitchen.
D In the kitchen, good. You were crawling on the floor . . . and now
. . . what's happening?
J I'm pulling myself up on a chair.
D Is anyone with you?
J Yes . . . Mummy's there.
D What colour is her dress? You can see.
J She's . . . she's not wearing a dress. She's wearing jeans.
D What's Mummy doing?
J She's holding her hands out.
D What's she saying?
J 'Who's a clever girl then.'
D When you need to know how things really were . . . and how they

are . . . how to see and assess your options . . . you now know where to go. You are claiming your birthright . . . the right to expand your consciousness . . . to be exceptional . . . to excel.

So . . . come back to now bringing that feeling of achievement with you and go to another time . . . another time of success, of personal achievement . . . it can be anything you like . . . keep the details to yourself . . . but choose an experience that gave you a great feeling of personal success . . . and make it one in which other people shared . . . in which other people were justifiably proud of you, happy for you . . . and nod your head when you've got it. Got one?

J Yes. (*Smiling*).

D Give me a keyword from it – a name, a place or a date – something that will immediately trigger the memory of that success.

J 'Degree'.

D Good . . . now do the same for love . . . loving and being loved.

J 'Paul'.

D Now one for self-confidence . . . confidence and competence.

J 'Train'.

D What other resource would you like to emphasize in yourself?

J Feeling happy.

D Fine . . . choose a time when you had a holiday feeling . . . you earned it . . . and you've got it! Free to enjoy yourself . . . free to enjoy life, to have fun. Or choose someone you know who radiated happiness . . . remember . . . you have the same resources to call upon . . . all waiting to find expression in your own life. Got one?

J Yes. 'Italy'.

D All right. You can add more, you can change the keywords as you see fit. But right now, I'm going to say 'Degree . . . Paul . . . Train . . . Italy' . . . how does that feel?

J Feels good. (*More smiles*).

D Now, this time, as I say the keywords – clench and then relax your dominant hand . . . your right hand . . 'Degree . . . Paul . . . Train . . . Italy' . . . creative mindset . . . set to positive feelings . . . set to how you choose to feel. Now, this time, repeat the keywords to yourself . . . and clench, and double the feeling, and relax. (*Smiles . . . nods*). Feels good? You don't need to tell me!

Now . . . any time you are confronted with a challenge in the future, you know what to do – just call on your resources, your mindpower. They're **there** . . . they're **there**. Know it . . . and be discreet. The gloomcasters and those who mislead and manipulate through promoting fear and shame and guilt and self-doubt would rather not know. You see, knowing how to rely on yourself . . . you don't need them. Just accept you had something to learn . . . be grateful . . . and move on to still greater things! Only that way, do you become strong . . . you evolve as an individual.

Now, let me paint you a picture and if it starts to disturb you . . . choose one of your keywords . . . and see what happens next.

(*When I tested Joan's responses initially on biofeedback, asking her to choose someone who really upset her, she chose her boss . . . the needle shot to the full extent of the high stress register. I painted a picture of a heavy office problem. Joan is a secretary . . . and Joan clenched and opened her hand – and smiled*).

How did that feel?

J   No problem!

D   Easy, isn't it? It's a raja yoga technique, perhaps five thousand years old . . . relatively new!

And you will find you can expand on it and soon . . . and much sooner than you think . . . the resources will be available to you quite spontaneously. You only have to **initiate** the process . . . subcon does the rest. Spontaneous right action . . . success on tap.

Now just relax as I confirm that subcon knows that you have had eight treatments of chemotherapy recently and that this is the best that can be offered with the present level of medical understanding. A triple dose of chemotherapy is scheduled in a month's time, subject to a further scan.

In view of the urgency of the situation, subcon . . . can you confirm that the effectiveness of the healing will be apparent to the medical experts involved and that their tests will confirm that Joan's bodymind system is entirely clear of cancer – is fully healed . . .? And you have your answer, Joan – affirmative. Thank you subcon . . . appreciated.

You see, Joan . . . the point is that until you are consciously alerted as to how the self-limiting negative conditioning was seeded, you lack the ability to contribute consciously to correcting the errors in internal communication . . . and all levels of mind, seemingly, must be involved. As soon as you see the cause, the desirable behavioural patterns can be imprinted on the appropriate brain cells and the natural healing processes are automatically stimulated. Whatever the problem . . . and this includes severe brain damage . . . the capacity of the bodymind system for correction is entirely unlimited . . . the urge of the cells and the control system is **always** lifewards. The lesson of the greatest mindmasters has always been the same . . . 'Simplify yourself' . . .

drop your negative conditioning. Self-healing through self-discovery is the simple name of the healing game. You don't have to believe anything, you just have to find out for yourself.

(*The closing sequence followed, as detailed in PS5*).

During the closing sequence, the client in this case was uncommonly animated and communicative. Uncommonly, because at this stage the client is usually happy to relax and listen. One client described his feelings as being a mixture of elation and exhaustion similar to knowing that he had just won a marathon . . . combined with the feeling, this time, that he would like to do it all over again.

With Joan, elation was also the stronger emotion and she interrupted my fairly routine closing sequence several times.

D . . . you'll be more poised and serene, more loving and loved than ever before and this sense of poise and love and serenity will stay with you and grow and those things . . .

J Yes!! Yes!! There **is** something else! I can see how I separated myself from my mother.

D Yes?

J Yes. I think I could perfectly well let the love flow back. Properly, not half-heartedly. I know she will still irritate me in the same way.

D Perhaps not. She will tend to act in the same way, because she is caught in her conditioning. Understanding that – because you were caught in yours – you will respond to her in a different way. When one of you changes . . . the game changes.

J Yes . . . and she will change . . . I can see how already. One of her favourites is to call it rebellion if I disagree with her. 'Remember' she says, 'that I am your mother. Honour thy father and thy mother . . . that's God's command.'

D A great one that! Commercialised religions are riddled with similar shallow-minded concepts. Their basic error is the concept of duality . . . separateness . . . them and us, saints and sinners, godheads and devils, heaven and hell. Then the duality is conveniently forgotten in 'honour your father and mother' . . . **if they are worthy of honour**. 'Forgive them, for they don't know what they do'. Nonsense. They know very well what they do. What they don't know is how they were conditioned to behave as they do. And incidentally, whether it is better to give or receive is irrelevant, except as evidence of a confused mind. The real trick in life is choosing those with whom it is enjoyable to share. Knowing yourself, you know how to choose . . . you can only succeed!

J Yes!

D Let me hear it then: 'I can only succeed'.

J I . . . only succeed.

D Tentative . . . Convince me!

J I think I . . . oh no! I see it . . . all my life I have programmed myself to failure. I have always expected the worst (*sobbing*).

D So . . . you were very successful in failing.

J Very . . . very successful. (*Chuckling*).

D . . . and now you will succeed in whatever you decide to tackle.

J I will succeed then . . . yes . . . (*contemplative*).

D Convince me.

J I will suc-**ceed**.

D Didn't hear you.

J **I will suc-ceed!** (*Laughing*).

D What was that?

J **I will suc-ceed!!!**

D **Right!!!** . . . and there's just one person who can guarantee you do . . . and you're it!

Stay with that understanding and at the count of five . . . (*wake-up routine*).

Later News . . . A first and second scan confirmed that the cancer had cleared. The lady consultant's comment on the first scan was: 'This is impossible . . . the tumour must be somewhere.'

Joan telephoned some time later: 'You won't believe this. Mother and I went on holiday to Majorca together . . . we had great fun. We behaved like a couple of teenagers.'

Joan is now an effective healer-therapist. She dealt successfully with her first brain-tumour case in three hours.

Case Summaries

Case 1: Woman client, 44, twice divorced, diagnosed as manic-depressive, little self-confidence. Ideodynamics indicated a birth trauma. Next step?

Case 2: Woman client, 30, anorexic. Major compounding event, sexually molested in a garden hut at the age of five. Her five-year-old playmate ran for help and her mother (surprisingly) found a handy policewoman. They entered the hut and the policewoman questioned the gardener and the child. Throughout the story, no great emotion was displayed. Next step?

Case 3: Young woman, attempted suicide. Parents favoured cleverer, prettier sister. A compounding event, at the age of four, involved hearing her mother's friend saying: 'How strange she is such a plain little thing, with such a beautiful sister.' Attempted suicide . . . reflected? Next step?

Case 4: Nurse, aware that she needed a change of career, possibly within the nursing profession but unclear as to her options. Called on subcon to clarify her options . . . which it did in 30 seconds. Facial expressions indicated she was surprised . . . and delighted. She preferred not to discuss them but wanted to know how she could be sure to choose the right one for her . . . subcon had provided two options. Next step?

Case 5: 'How do I know that my feelings of inadequacy won't come back? Your response?

Case 6: Man, 60, hard-working executive, tinnitus for fifteen years and mastoid discharge problems. Too impatient for relief to use the tinnitus tape. In therapy, amusingly used both hands to see if he could open his eyes when asked to test for relaxation. On a scale of zero to ten, reported that the then-present ringing volume was eight and he had difficulty in hearing. First step? Second step? Third step?

Case 7:   Man, 45, acrophobic. A movie photographer, his job was at risk. Analysis revealed a compounding event at the age of four. A cousin held him over a bannister by the heels. Subcon revealed the I.S.E. at six months. He was in his mother's arms when she nearly fell over a cliff. Next question?

Case 8:   Woman client, 40, asthma, diabetes. Client reported that she had been greatly helped with her asthma problem (and itching at night) by a non-European doctor. She was unable to maintain physical relaxation. Next step?

Case 9:   Woman client, 52. Presenting symptom, overweight, depressed, etc. Analysis traced the comfort-eating habit to the age of three when her mother left to become a partisan. When the mother was reunited with the child, she had changed . . . she no longer seemed like her mother. The feelings expressed were insecurity and abandonment but there was no emotional release. Later events linked to feelings about the mother, again without much emotion. Subcon was asked to provide a meaningful word for the feeling.
           'Trembling' . . . next step?

Case 10:   Woman client, 42, single mother, four sons. Therapy was requested for her youngest son but the mother requested a short demonstration. In a matter of moments, she regressed to an event at the age of two. A woman put a baby in her arms and said: 'Hold him while I get his bottle.'
           Client: 'He **wriggled**! I've dropped him . . . and she's screaming at me?' Link to later life events?

Case 11:   Man, 52, in and out of care for thirty years for 'molesting' babies. His compulsion was, in fact, to pick them up and cuddle them. The initial sensitising event was at the age of nine months. Likely type of sensitising event?

Case 12:   Man, 44, pancreatic cancer. Analysis revealed the inevitable serious shocks and there was time to 'anchor' a few resources: loving feelings, success, etc. For success . . . the client chose the keywords: 'Nat Pro' . . . and was clearly happy about it. He telephoned several months later to report that he had no health problems but that he was experiencing unusual difficulties in his business. I remembered that he had volunteered in a pre-analysis chat that his greatest asset was his ability to persuade banks to provide finance for his businesses, several of which had failed. Suggestion to the client?

Case 13: One-time doctor (general practitioner), 82, interested in hypnoanalysis. The client had used relaxation techniques when treating patients and he fully recovered from bowel cancer, attributing the healing to a macrobiotic diet. Analysis confirmed that he had no physiological problems. The Lüscher test indicated stress four, and an ANS imbalance. For amusement, he requested a 'previous life' regression. He saw himself watching a prison ship leaving for Australia with all his best friends aboard and he experienced a profound sense of loss. The message he got?

Case 14: Woman client, 44, lesbian, menopausal. Visible heart palpitations aggravated by HRT. Anchoring success, the client chose: 'Knock 'em for dead' . . . acceptable anchor?

Case 15: Woman, 43, married, hospitalised and in a medical coma. Five weeks on *diamorphine* (whimpering sounds were thought to be due to pain) and *phenytoin*, seemingly standard treatment. A side-effect was diarrhoea and, as the walls of the bowels and the uterus had become perforated, the mode of discharge was unusual. Action?

Case 16: Woman, 35, inoperable brain tumor. The lady was swollen to double her normal size with steroids to the extent that her face was expressionless . . . the facial muscles were too weak to allow her to smile. The nature of the presenting symptom mitigated against using feelings as a bridge to the sensitising and compounding events. Process?

Case 17: Man, 38, violently jealous, wife-basher and with several other serious emotional problems. Accompanied by his common-law wife, both visiting the UK from abroad, they attended for four-hours' therapy. (For one reason or another I usually refer a partner or relative to another therapist).

As an embryo, the man was aware that his mother was leaving him as soon as he was born. Her husband had been overseas for several years. He knew the solitude of being an illegitimate half-caste. Many factors compounded his jealousy and violent behaviour. Six problems were cleared in therapy with heavy abreactions and biofeedback confirmed that stress levels were reduced to below British average. Next step?

Case 18: African doctor, had spent nearly £2,000 to be trained in hypnotherapy by a popular therapist in London but felt that he had never been hypnotised. Responded well to induction but opened his eyes at phase three (Esdaile state). Action?

Case 19: Woman client living in dread of illness and the possibility of needing further medical treatment. She was consciously aware of her premature birth and the death, in hospital, of her three-year-old brother. He had polio but this was diagnosed as appendicitis and he was operated on for that. Regression revealed that she was born with pneumonia and overheard a statement that she was unlikely to live a week. Leg problems at four linked to an authoritative comment that she would be in a wheelchair later in life. Her maternal grandmother died of cancer when my client was five. A doctor remarked that everyone has cancer cells in the body and that the disease could strike anyone. Finally, an abcess on her forehead at seven was deemed likely to have caused brain damage . . . she overheard a doctor reporting this to her mother. Action?

Case 20: Nurse, 33, single, diagnosed as manic depressive. Lüscher stress-level ten. Highly unresponsive, apathetic. Birth trauma, mother not eating well . . . client did not want to be born. Next step?

Case 21: Woman, 28, no self-confidence etc. Birthing experience . . . did not want to be born. Next step?

Case 22: Doctor, 48, water phobia. Could not board a boat. Sat bolt upright, eyes staring and screamed like a banshee when counted down to relax. Next step?

Case 23: Male nurse, 40, presenting symptom, lack of fulfilment and success. At phase three, spelled out his major problem as 'sexual'. Nature? 'Homosexual'. Next question . . .?

Case 24: Single mother, 40, bowel cancer. Attended for precision analysis on a Sunday, having spent the previous five or six days at a cancer help centre. (The following weeks she visited a macrobiotic diet centre). She had responded well to the three 'Cancel Cancer' tapes. A Lüscher retest before her visit indicated renewed hope, energy, willpower . . . the ingredients for success. Unlike several cancer clients who had visited that particular help centre, she had not been intentionally or unintentionally conditioned to resist conscious self-hypnosis inductions. After five days of 'let's-all-have-a-jolly-time-with-our-cancer-together' . . . she was clearly euphoric. Analysis procedure?

Case 25: Boy, aged four, diabetes for one year, insulin dependent. Afraid of the daily injections. Extremely restless. Eyes opened constantly, glancing left to ensure that his mother was still present. Action?

Case 26: Successful entrepreneur, man, 48, divorced four times. Presenting problem, unable to sustain love. (Lüscher read 1 2 3 4 5 6 7 0 twice and gave a valuable clue).

Client was consciously aware that he was a foundling child, dumped by his mother at the age of six months. Amongst other things, his personality had become moulded around the concept that nobody could love him for long . . . he expected to be dumped. Action?

Case 27: Only child, 43, panic attacks, on tranquillisers for over twenty years, eight operations including a hysterectomy. (She had not seen a doctor for several years. Her prescription for *Premarin* and *Valium* had been automatically renewed on visiting the clinic). The client showed no emotional response to the rebirthing script. Next question?

Case Results

Case 1: *Birth script. Client was dumped/discarded at birth as attention was focused on her twin, who was stillborn. Guilt feelings were compounded by her mother's attitudes. Unable to sustain close relationships, her two marriages were . . . short-lived.*

Case 2: *'The policewoman has just arrived . . . what are you telling her?' A strong emotional release followed. The child had lied to the policewoman, saying that nothing had happened. It was the lie, not the sexual abuse, that created the damaging repression.*

Case 3: *'Attempted' suicide . . . a serious emotional leverage game . . . emotional blackmail. In this case, the culmination of a lifetime of 'gameplaying' to attract attention. Unresponsive . . . though clearly interested in the 'mechanics' of therapy and happy that her parents were paying the fee. 'Foxing the analyst' was also clearly part of a new game . . . she had been to several other therapists. Her game, in other words, had taken over the gameplayer.*

First attempt to reach the 'child within' failed completely. There was a distinct similarity between this 'barrier' state and working with someone in a medical coma. The client responded within five minutes to a subliminal 'coma access' tape and analysis was successfully completed. A modified version of the tape has proved useful in similar cases in which manipulative gameplaying has become a way of life or where apathy rules.

Case 4: *'Focus on one of the options . . . I'll call that one Option Green. Focus on the other option . . . I'll call that one Option Blue. As each one is different, it will reflect a different feeling somewhere in the bodymind system . . . notice where the feeling is when I say "Option Green" – at the count of three . . . 1 . . . 2 . . . 3 . . .* **option green.** *Got it? Good feeling? Now I'll ask subcon to* *provide the same intensity of feeling somewhere else in the body for Option Blue . . . 1 . . . 2 . . . 3 . . .* **option blue**. *Got it? Great. Now watch this. At the count of three, subcon will double the feeling for a moment in the area reflecting your best option . . . 1 . . . 2 . . . 3. Got it? "Blue". There's your option . . . dedicate to it.'*

Case 5: *Right now, you don't know, or you wouldn't have asked me the question. You have still to overcome your last enemy . . . self-doubt. You know how to initiate process . . . use it, until it stimulates spontaneous right action. You bypass the mind that thinks and doubts, you function from the mind that knows . . . you develop your insight, your intuition . . . quite automatically. You learn to trust in yourself, your truth. Time comes when you transcend the mind that knows . . . you function from a source of wisdom. It is in you now but it is obscured from view, hidden behind all your questions. Have you any other questions for subcon?*

Case 6: *An imaginary volume control was 'installed' grading internal sound levels from ten (loud) to zero. The client was shown how to reduce the internal sound to zero. It was then increased and the client reduced it to zero. Next step . . . analysis. Compounding events included being hit on the head by a teacher and stopping a cricket ball with his forehead. The initial sensitising event was awareness of his parents shouting at one another when he was a six-month-old foetus. Shouting turned out to be the link between all past and recent events. Third step . . . ensuring that shouting no longer triggered the internal 'blocking'.*

Case 7: *'Where is your father?' He managed to grab the mother. Apparently, her intention had been to jump.*

Case 8: *Use a hypnotic seal-breaking technique. The client has apparently been 'sealed-off' either intentionally or by accident. It took two minutes to cancel the seal. The asthma sensitivity was seeded at birth (the most common occurence) . . . and the itching originated when she was tightly bound in a rough blanket by her grandmother at the age of one. The client reported that she had also lost her fear of flying . . . which had not been mentioned as being a concern.*

Case 9: *Confirmed that 'trembling' was the feeling as a child . . . when* *mother left, etc. Various incidents again produced little emotion. A suggestion to go to a recent event produced a strong abreaction. 'Mother lives with us now. Every time I look at her I'm wishing her dead . . . I feel evil.' (In the induction process, the client had been unable to let numbers go to achieve phase two relaxation . . . she counted 97 . . . 96 . . . 95 etc.). 'Right . . . just relax and count backwards from 100 and at 97 . . . just let the numbers fade away.' The client again counted 100 . . . 99 . . . 98 . . . 97 . . . 96 . . . 95 . . . 'Stop! You see . . . you are not in control of your thoughts . . . so how can you feel guilty about them? Now, let me show you how to go to where YOU are in charge.'*

Case 10: *'I can see it! I'm always left holding the baby.'*

Case 11: *His home came under enemy attack and he was the sole survivor.*

Case 12: *The suggestion was to link his 'success' keyword to an event in which he and others had prospered . . . not one in which he had been smart at the expense of others. It worked! Though it can be made clear in therapy that the client does not have to describe the successful event, it is advisable to suggest that the client chooses one in which everyone involved either shared in the success or was proud of it. 'Prosper all' is the happier theme.*

Case 13: *When the doctor went 'holistic' some twenty years ago, he lost his doctorate and his professional friends. He was unable to 'reach' them – their minds were imprisoned. He had, however, successfully contrived to hide the deep sense of loss and injustice that he felt. He was amazed at the real sense of relief and release that he felt.*

Case 14: *When I repeated 'Knock 'em for dead', the client laughed heartily. Until then, emotional expression had been absent. Conscious of my earlier anchoring experience, I asked for an explanation. Apparently, when she and her flat-mates dressed to go dancing . . . this was their favourite expression of mutual admiration. Therapy moved forward well from then on.*

Case 15: *The Esdaile 'coma' state (Phase Three) is ideal for natural childbirth and conditions normally requiring anaesthesia. Deeper states, in which the state of creative insight is further elevated, can also be induced (to Phase Seven and beyond). The Pilgrim medical coma-access tape is based on experience of 'working' at* *these elevated states. The tape was playing for several hours before I arrived at the hospital. Ideomotor signals were installed and doubly checked. To my first question 'Do you wish to return to everyday living reality?' the response was 'Yes' . . . and 'No'. It took nearly two hours to learn, step-by-step, the events leading up to choosing the coma state as a refuge. The movement of the left foot and left hand indicated 'Yes' and 'No'. Questioning confirmed the medical impression that a stroke had paralysed the right hand and foot. Ensuring that the client wanted her husband to know the whole story took further time. Fortunately (as a Lüscher test revealed before I conveyed how the client's scheming had backfired suddenly) the husband was one of those rare, loving, emotionally mature men . . . in my experience, one of only three in a hundred. He readily established ideomotor communication and together they dealt with the relationship problems. The client came out of coma within two days.*

In this and subsequent cases, indications are that the medical coma state is chosen as a refuge by people who are emotionally sensitive, vulnerable and immature and who have no strong back-up style. If their childish charm fails to work . . . they drop out. The hospital staff were very cooperative, even to the extent of listing the side-effects of the diamorphine *and* phenytoin. *They expressed interest in the information that, even if the patient is screaming, it represents an attempt to communicate and is not a signal of pain. Though they were impressed by the simplicity of the coma release technique, they explained that they were unable to adopt it.*

Case 16: *Established first-class ideodynamic signalling and asked subcon if ideodynamic responses, witness and ego-state processes could be used to accelerate restoration of the bodymind system to healthy functioning, free from the problem we identify as a brain tumor. (Affirmative). Also confirmed that there is no malignancy in the bodymind system or in Nature . . . obedience to faulty signals was causing the defensive measure of creating what we identify as a tumour. No other ego-state was apparently involved. Analysis more or less followed the lines of the case reported in full and 'going inside' revealed that the tumour had cleared in eight weeks. (A scan four weeks later revealed that it had gone). Focusing on the more serious problem, I omitted to deal specifically with the effects of the steroid treatment. The lady, who lives remote from Shrewsbury, was restored to normal size over a period of months, possibly assisted by the 'post-*

*operation sensitivities' tape. This tape has proved helpful over a
wide range of problems, from post-operation itching and pain to
numbness and immobility.*

Case 17: *Stress was low enough for the client to use NRG+, a post-
analysis abreactive tape, to clear out any remaining self-limiting
negative conditioning . . . together with 'Serenity ECS' (enhanced coping skills) to harmonise all levels of mind and being.
The client knew that the emotional trauma was better out than in
and the after-effect was relief and release. Two months later, he
telephoned to explain that he was free from all his old problems.
A heavily repressed event, involving his mother's reaction when
he traced her and visited her at the age of twelve, produced an
abreaction heavier than all the earlier ones. The mother had
encouraged her legal husband to assault her illegitimate son,
both physically and sexually.*

Case 18: *Reinduced to phase three, asked to try to bend his index finger,
right hand . . . the doctor did so. Using the simplest seal-breaking process, in less than three minutes the client was so relaxed
that he clearly experienced reluctance to move to a suitably light
working level. The seal dated from the age of six, when his father
trained him to disregard the influence of the village witchdoctor
by mentally cancelling everything he said. The seal lasted thirty
years. An interesting point is that the client's stress levels had
dropped from Lüscher scale eight to two in the eight weeks before
his appointment. He had reported discomfort in dozing or sleeping to the hypnosis side of three simple, non-abreactive tapes.
Presumably, the subliminal versions alone were effective.*

Case 19: *Reminded the client that each prediction had been false. Had the
client 'go inside' to check for any serious defects or deficiencies.
There were none. Subcon was asked to provide a date by which a
minor shoulder injury would be healed. The date chosen was only
ten days ahead. The client reported all clear on the due date,
imagination working happily for her instead of against her.*

Case 20: *Move the feeling forward to the next time. Mother's religious
understanding was that life was a punishment, death was release. Later events in hospitals compounded the influence, result-
ing in the apathy. 'Allowed' her to hear what others would say
about her 'lifestyle' after her death . . . and asked subcon to
provide two options. She is now making a career outside the
hospital atmosphere.*

Case 21: *'You didn't want to be born because . . .?' 'Because I wasn't READY.' She had been told that her birth was premature and that consequently she was not properly formed. Her lack of success was attributed to the 'fact' that she was defective or deficient in some respect. Subcon confirmed that she was a breech birth . . . that she was only four days premature . . . that she was fully and correctly formed.*

Case 22: *Became deeply relaxed when asked to see himself rise above his body and fly high above the clouds. He was then asked to take himself down deeply into relaxation. He did so. In response to: 'A word will spring to mind to link you to the initial sensitising event . . .' he gagged. 'Birth water!' Next event, aged four . . . head rolled back as he spluttered 'Bath water.' His six-year-old sister was attempting to bath him. A week after the therapy session, a picture postcard of Lake Constance arrived from the client with the message: 'Turns out I love boats and water.'*

Case 23: *'Do you want to be heterosexual?' 'Yes.' Next question: 'Do you have a friend who will resent losing you as a sex partner?' It was explained that we all have the ability to choose and we only need to know how to initiate the process of change. In many cases, the desire for change is limited to knowing how the homosexuality arose and how life as a homosexual can be enhanced. This was the case here. Age-regression revealed that both the mother and father wanted a daughter to replace a stillborn child. The client was treated as a girl from birth, even to the extent of being dressed in the stillborn girl's clothes. Barriers to success and fulfilment were dealt with in analysis and later reports confirmed that a satisfactory career change had been made. Relationships improved to the extent that the client's partner attended for a similar 'fact-finding and self-understanding' analysis.*

Case 24: *Experienced in dealing effectively with clients locked into unreasoned fears and depression, I failed to break through the equally unbalanced mental/emotional state of false optimism. The various forms of false comfort she had accepted presented a formidable barrier to analysis . . . a barrier that I failed, in this case, to penetrate. The client left in the same euphoric state in which she had arrived. I learned of her death two months later. As many analysts have discovered, similar cases tend to occur within days or weeks of one another. In two later cases, breaking through the aura of self-delusion and false comfort only involved* *regressing the clients to their first day at school to establish a sensible working climate for effective analysis and healing.*

Case 25: *Induce the sleep-attached-to-hynosis state and endeavour to learn the causal factor, etc., not necessarily to be brought to the young lad's consciousness. The mother, an experienced therapist, was coached in working with the lad, through the medium of ideodynamics, while he was asleep. A periodic reduction in insulin, unit by unit, was coordinated with subcon, ensuring that subcon agreed to increase the natural production of insulin step-by-step to compensate. Insulin dependence was gradually reduced to half and a subliminal tape was provided to stimulate further improvement.*

Case 26: *Rebirthing script. A dramatic shift in understanding occurred on seeing that he was abandoned a few hours after his birth . . . not after six months, as he had been told. The difference? His mother had not dumped him because he was unlovable.*

Case 27: *'Was it pre-birth?' (Yes). 'As an embryo?' (No). 'As a foetus?' (No). 'In a previous life experience?' (No). (Light blossomed!) 'Was it at conception?' (Yes). Further questions revealed that the mother was the victim of a rapist who had almost killed her. I thought to ask: 'Strangled?' to which the response was 'Yes.' 'Were all the five-to seven-million eggs in the mother's womb shocked?' (Yes). The client's mother had told her that her father had left them when the daughter was only six months old. She later telephoned to say that her mother had now confirmed the truth. She never knew her attacker. Her mother married but had no further children.*

Question Time

1. Each phase of the induction having been completed effectively and tested . . . what is the next suggestion?

2. How do you get a verbal indication of how deeply relaxed the client feels?

3. If a client fails to 'go down' deeply to a countdown procedure, what can you do?

4. Some clients may feel that they cannot visualise properly. How do you convince them that they can?

5. The client has described his needs and is now creatively relaxed. Your next objective in analysis?

6. Assuming a client has described his problem as depression, anxiety, lack of success, inability to sustain loving relationships, jealousy etc., what should you seek to know?

7. The client reports that he feels nothing. Next step?

8. When should you seek to establish ideodynamic signalling?

9. You seek to establish Phase Two (mental) relaxation sugesting that the client count backwards from 100, letting the numbers go at 97 . . . he continues to count. Next suggestion?

10. You check the client's arm and confirm that it is fully relaxed. Next step?

11. You need time to decide on your next move. What do you do?

12. You decide to find if there is another ego-state involved, even though there is no evidence of schizophrenia. Why can this sometimes be helpful?

13. You choose to trace the client's name on the back of his hand with your fingertip and, with three strokes of the finger, erase it from his hand and erase it from his thoughts. You than ask: 'What did I trace on your hand?' Purpose?

14. Some therapists encounter clients who feel that they were never hypnotised. How do you pre-empt this?

15. You use a simple age regression technique to take the client to the first time he walked or to his first day at school. With what purpose?

16. How do you ensure that you are alerted to any discomfort that the client may be experiencing?

17. What is the test for Phase Three relaxation – the basement or near-Esdaile state?

18. What working level is useful for children in analysis?

19. How do you determine the resources and the coping skills that your client needs?

20. How do you stimulate or reinforce a client's skills and resources?

21. How do you test the beneficial influence of suggestions that have been anchored?

22. How would you apply the pinpointing process (assuming you chose it) to deal with a simple malady . . . asthma for example?

23. Regressing to an event, you ask the client . . . 'are you alone or with someone?' The client is hesitant in response. Next question?

24. How do you interpret your client's dreams?

25. At the end of a therapy session, you decide to future-pace the client seven days ahead. With what purpose?

26. In healing, it is essential to obtain forgiveness . . . to get rid of all ill-feelings, though not necessarily to excuse. Why forgive?

27. You encounter a reluctance on the part of the client to disclose something. Next step?

28. Your client says that he feels different about something. How do you prompt him to clarify his position?

29. Assuming that your client is physically relaxed and the critical faculty has been bypassed, how do you further deepen the state of creative relaxation?

30. Your client has spelled out a word that subcon has provided to link to his greatest problem area. Next step?

31. How do you help a client to determine his best options in life?

32. You explain to a client that the four fundamental life needs are at the vibrational level of reality. How do you determine the client's position in these?

33. The client's problem, let us say, is a skin complaint, itching. You decide to use the affect bridge technique to find out how the problem originated. How?

34. When does the 'gestalting' process (resolving unfinished psychic business by achieving a 'closure') come in useful in analysis?

35. In failing to live up to our own or someone else's expectations ... what is the common error that must be recognised and corrected?

36. The doctrinaire belief is that a spontaneous remission is a freak occurence ... something that happens, cause unknown. How is a 'spontaneous remission' caused?

37. Is it always essential to confirm the truth of what a client reveals when he is at a 'working level' of conscious hypnosis?

38. A client, who is recovering from dental or medical treatment, telephones to seek temporary relief from severe pain. What do you say to him?

39. A friend or relation of a client telephones to report that the client has suffered a strong emotional reaction and her doctor has injected her against convulsions ... what do you say?

40. Your client is thoroughly relaxed and you ask for a response at the count of three ... 'one ... two ... three ...' and you click your fingers to focus attention ... the client responds with a noticeable start or nervous twitch. Next step?

41. A client releases repressed emotions involving sexual abuse as a child or evidence of manipulative 'gameplaying' tactics which have persisted to today. You devote time to ego-boosting and to dealing effectively with secondary benefits and you request subcon to provide the client with more suitable options, fully aware that dependence on the analyst may otherwise become part of the game. Next step?

42. You establish with subcon what resources are needed to achieve the client's best option. Next step?

43. Your client is in pain or has tinnitus or influenza or some other disability that could act as a distraction during analysis. How do you ease the problem, temporarily?

44. A suicidal client is referred to you or you detect suicidal tendencies in a pre-therapy Lüscher test. You ensure?

45. A client has blossomed as heavy repressions were satisfactorily identified and released. Prescribed drugs and narcotics have been part of the daily diet. The client asks if they should now be dropped. Your response?

46. You are handed a list of twenty problems the client would like to resolve. How do you decide which to tackle first and also ensure that all the client's needs are effectively met?

47. The problem involves pain and discomfort in some area, say an arthritic knee. Having temporarily switched off the discomfort and then identified and released the causal and compounding factors . . . what is a worthwhile next step?

48. A client is concerned that she may have to endure a sixth breast cancer operation. Her company has recently failed, her husband has left her, her home has been repossessed. A Lüscher test confirms that her stress level is very high. She has three children to support. Your fee for the three to four hours precision therapy she will require is normally £500. What will you tell her?

49. An effective abreaction can be evidenced by a strong mental, emotional and physical release. How long can it take to clear an abreaction thoroughly?

50. What technique would you suggest to demonstrate the hypnoanalytical process publicly or to analyse a close friend or relative?

51. How do you confirm that the client is in a state of conscious self-hypnosis?

52. What are the indications that effective ideomotor signalling has been established?

53. As part of your completion suggestions, you advise your client that the two-way communication channel with subcon will always be available to him when required . . . and you want to ensure that he has no doubts about the fact that he has been deeply relaxed. How?

54. You are taking a client down to the basement level of relaxation (Phase Three), going down on a lift or escalator from, say, floor three. The client says that he feels as though he is going up. Next step?

55. The client seems to have entered a state of aphasia, a stupor in which he is reluctant to talk. (This can happen when the client has unwittingly been in a state of tension for months or years). Next step?

56. You regress the client to an earlier event and ask . . . 'are you indoors or outdoors?' . . . and get no response. Next question?

57. A client is accompanied by a friend or family member who is clearly under some stress. With a few minutes available, what can you offer to do?

58. Your lady client is sitting comfortably with her legs crossed as you start to induce relaxation. How?

59. In your completion suggestions, you ask subcon to ensure that your client is motivated to make whatever beneficial changes are required in his thinking habits and behavioural patterns. Next step?

60. A client is clearly engaged in a game of emotional leverage with his wife. He declares that he just wants to be dead. Action?

61. Why do you, as the analyst, experience the same sense of exhilaration – of mental and emotional intimacy – as your client when his repressed negativity is released?

62. In precision therapy, how do you ensure that your work is fully effective and free from the attachment, resistance and transference problems associated with earlier forms of analysis?

63. Your problems are all in the mind. Correct?

64. What is the purpose in offering to take a client through a previous life experience when, as an experienced analyst, you feel that cryptomnesia or some other form of self-delusion may be involved?

Suggested Responses

1. While we are working together for the benefit of your entire bodymind system, you will automatically relax creatively whenever I ask you to move to Phase Three and you will also find that from now on you will automatically gain access to levels one, two or three whenever it is appropriate for you to do so merely by mentally repeating Phase One, Phase Two or Phase Three or whatever private keywords you decide to choose . . . and subcon will always ensure that the phase of relaxation you attain is appropriate for the occasion.

2. As you continue to relax with your eyes comfortably closed – just imagine that you can see a ruler marked ten at the top and zero at the bottom . . . ten representing wide awake and zero representing deeply relaxed . . . where would you say you are on the ruler? That's good . . . what colour is the ruler? The numbers on the ruler . . . what colour are they? Good.

3. Now just imagine you can rise above your body and go right through the ceiling and rise up above the rooftops . . . and go even higher . . . looking down at the clouds . . . all white in the sunlight . . . see the towns and the countryside, the mountains and the rivers, the valleys and fields . . . and come back to now, back through the clouds and through the roof and the ceiling and back to your body and notice how wonderful it feels just to relax . . . as I count you down from eight to zero, go ten times more deeply relaxed.

4. I'm going to ask you three questions, and just nod your head if the answer is 'yes' . . . do you know what a telephone looks like? An elephant? A television set? That's visualising . . . the word conveys the picture to the control mind. You can practise creating mental three-dimensional images if you have time to waste. In healing with conscious self-hypnosis . . . the word conveys.

5. To bypass the mind-levels that 'think' or 'know' (the monkey-

mind, the superficial conscious linear-conditioned levels of mind) . . . bypassing 'memory' and gaining access to the control levels that can re-experience events.

6. Where, in the body, is the feeling?

7. When I raise and lower your arm . . . you will notice a feeling somewhere in your body associated with the problem . . . (raise and drop the arm: 'Where's the feeling?') . . .

   Or . . . at the count of three, subcon will induce the feeling . . . **or** . . . use any of the processes for dealing with 'nothing' responses presented elsewhere in the therapy sessions notes.

8. As soon as possible.

9. As I raise and lower your arm, say . . . 'Numbers go' . . . and the numbers are gone completely!

   Or: Count after me . . . 96 . . . 95 . . . 93 . . . 90 . . . 87 . . . 85 – next number? Good . . . now watch the numbers fade – you can bring thoughts into your consciousness . . . now . . . just tell them to go . . . put yourself in charge of your thoughts. Just relax as I count you down from eight to zero . . . 8 . . . doubling your state of relaxation . . . 7 . . . relaxed, but more fully aware . . . 6 . . . more fully aware at the creative levels of consciousness . . . 5 . . . etc.

   It is not essential to establish Phase Two relaxation at the early stages . . . it helps greatly to do so.

10. Check the other arm. Ensure the client is physically relaxed. Ask: 'Is anything concerning you at the moment?' (You may have neglected to ask the client if a pre-therapy visit to the toilet is needed). Get relaxation and ask: 'Feel the difference now? Good!'

11. For the next sixty seconds . . . just relax and dream . . . and subcon will bring to mind an event or a feeling that has relevance to the cause of the problem . . . and ask: 'Where are you now in your thoughts?' before you proceed to the next step.

   As the client has no clear conception of the passage of time, focus on your next move without regard to whether the interval is more or less than sixty seconds.

12. Explaining that we all have many personality facets and some can assert themselves in a maladaptive fashion without us being conscious of their existence can permit the client to release guilt and other feelings without seeming to take the blame for the

causative event. The client can dissociate himself from the behaviour.

13. To verify that memory has now been bypassed. (Memory is usually faulty ... memory usually reconstructs. It relies on a linear process of thought and life is not lived in straight lines).

14. Ask the client to stiffen an index finger and then try to bend it. Explain that it is under subcon control and when he opens his eyes in a moment, he will find it will stay rigid ... he can move his hand, but his finger will continue to point stiffly ... and have him open his eyes ... look at his finger ... and find that it is no longer under conscious control.

'Close your eyes and allow the finger to relax.'

Or have the client forget his home address when he opens his eyes ... 'and now close your eyes and of course you can easily remember your address ... in fact your powers of recall will be ten times better than they have ever been from now on ... and you will be aware of that improvement.'

15. To demonstrate that the client has access to mind levels of greatly enhanced awareness.

16. Your subcon will alert me to any discomfort you may be experiencing by allowing your thumbs to waggle.

17. For analytical purposes, it is sufficient to verify that there is no physical response to a direct command to raise an arm.

18. The 'sleep-attached' state ... bypassing the child's consciousness to ensure that harmony and balance are appropriately maintained throughout the entire bodymind system. It is probably unnecessary but subcon can be requested to ensure that any distressing material that is contributing in any way to a problem is released and forgotten by the child immediately.

(Maturity in the adult enables us to attenuate the influence of unwelcome events. The 'subconscious' or more elevated mind levels are seemingly ageless).

19. Ask the client to dream for sixty seconds and bring them to mind.

20. Anchor the appropriate keywords (example in the session notes).

21. Future pace to the type of event that would have produced distress in the past.

22. You are now five years old . . . did you know what asthma was like then? Identify to an age or birthday then go back say, fifteen minutes before the asthmatic symptom was triggered and come forward through the event. (Example in the session notes.)

23. Have you been born yet?

24. Your conditioned mind is involved. Your interpretation is, at best, misleading and distractive. Use gestalt techniques or have the client see himself re-experiencing the dream, but this time, having subcon clarify the meaning.

25. Learn how the client has responded to the therapy . . . particularly how your generalisations have been successfully translated into specifics. Clearances will have been effected that were perhaps never revealed as problem areas.

26. All mental/emotional channels are seemingly two-way channels. The feelings you transmit reflect back on you.

    To blame anyone for their action is to blame them for their early conditioning. In the Zen experience, one understands that the education of a child starts one thousand years before it is born.

27. You can ask subcon if it is necessary to bring the matter to consciousness, with a tendency to invite a negative response. Ask the client if, with increased maturity and deeper understanding, the event can be discussed and released say, in five years time. (This is usually particularly acceptable to a young client). Future-pace five years and clear the impasse.

28. You feel different . . . because . . .?

    You avoid asking 'why' as this invites a 'don't know' response.

29. Practically anything that happens that is acceptable to the client will deepen the euphoric state, including the rustling of papers and loud traffic sounds. Several deepening techniques are listed in the session notes.

30. 'Now as I tap you on the forehead – put the word into a sentence.' Usually this suffices to effect the release of repressed material.

31. 'Relax and dream for sixty seconds.'

    Alternatively: 'Your subconscious control mind is fully aware of your best options at all times . . . of your 'next-greatest-good' . . . and in a moment, will bring it clearly to consciousness, not necessarily for discussion with me.' As I count now from three to zero and tap you gently on the forehead . . . the word will spring to mind that will serve to guide you to realisation of your best options in life (count, tap) . . . the word? Now this time: put the word into a sentence (tap) . . . got the message? Good . . . now relax and allow subcon to provide you with all the necessary details. Nod your head when you clearly understand what you need to do. (An alternative procedure is provided in the session notes).

32. On a scale of ten to zero, where ten represents excellence and zero represents lack . . . how do you feel now about your ability to act and succeed?

33. A feeling is experienced somewhere in the bodymind system that triggers the itching response. At the count of three, subcon will bring on that feeling strongly and you will be able to tell me what it is and where it is . . . 1 . . . 2 . . . 3 . . . (click) . . . Where's the feeling? How do you describe it? Now go back to 15 minutes before the first time that feeling was triggered, and tell me what is happening.

34. In giving the other people or things in a dream a voice so that they can be addressed and can respond . . . and 'writing the script' in dealing with relationship problems . . . for example: 'You are not a dependent child now . . . tell your father what you think of his behaviour towards his four-year-old daughter . . . What do you want to do to him? Do it . . . do it now! Give him a voice . . . let him explain his behaviour . . . etc. What did you really want to tell him? 'On the one hand I think this . . . on the other, I think that' . . . so talk to the other . . ., let's find if there is any common ground.'

35. Avoid the mistake of linking success or failure to self-worth.

36. A spontaneous remission is a dramatic shift in personal awareness that can readily be caused at a working level of conscious self-hypnosis, or even in our normal state of unconscious self-hypnosis.

37. Time and space and true or false are conditioned-mind concepts and part of our experience in the vibrational level of reality. They have no significance in healing. What is important is the psychic effect, consequently healing is instantaneous. In the same way, light can instantly dispel darkness that has reigned in a cave for thousands of years.

38. To the extent that you can do so comfortably . . . draw in a long, slow, deep breath . . . hold it . . . now blow the breath out by way of the mouth and feel the discomfort decrease. This time, as you breathe in, clench a fist and release as you blow the breath out . . . release still more of the discomfort . . . you will feel it go. Now this time, inhale, clench the fist, close your eyes and as you exhale . . . relax . . . open your eyes and the discomfort has practically gone . . . so repeat the process again . . . breath, fist, eyes closed and then exhale, relax . . . open your eyes and the discomfort has gone . . . and will not return for at least 24 hours . . . when you can repeat the process if it is needed . . . and notice how good you feel. (The simple mechanism of mindpower here is . . . want it to happen . . . know it can happen . . . it happens).

39. I am sure she will wish to contact me when she can.

40. Take the client back to the first time she was startled by a similar sound.

41. A strong double-sided subliminal tape is proving useful, particularly for 'sensitives' or highly dependent personalities, to enhance their day-to-day coping skills and help them to move more powerfully into the future. (Pilgrim Serenity ECS).

42. Ask: 'How do you feel about that now?' 'Wonderful.' 'No . . . that's a word . . . show me . . . how do you feel.' Double the feeling . . . anchor it to a keyword.

43. On a scale of zero to ten . . . where ten represents the worst discomfort . . . how do you feel now? (Ten) . . . 'Now just imagine there is a control knob that you can reach that controls the level of discomfort . . . and as I count down from nine to zero . . . see yourself turn the control knob down from ten to zero discomfort . . . 9 . . . 8 . . . 7 . . . feel the discomfort decrease . . . 6 . . . 5 . . . 4 . . . getting less and less . . . 3 . . . 2 . . . 1 . . . zero . . . and the discomfort is gone . . . gone completely . . . how do you feel?'

    (Ah . . . you have lost that relaxation . . . as I raise and lower your arm, all discomfort will go . . . there you are . . . just release, relax and let go . . .).

44. The client must have some responsible person to accompany him home and must complete a signed statement describing what he has been contemplating. The client's signature should be witnessed by the person who has accompanied him.

45. Drug-taking is a personal decision on which you do not

advise.Indications are that any withdrawal from drugs should be a gradual process. A freedom-from-drug-abuse tape is useful here.

46. Establish the real problems with subcon and deal with them in analysis, catering for general needs by anchoring resources. Future pace to test anchors and verify with subcon that all major problem areas have been resolved, all others to be dealt with through the natural medium of dreams and experiences, with the usual provisos.

47. Bring the mental sunlight down and focus on the area from within, comparing the tissue in the area of discomfort with the surrounding undamaged tissue . . . and in this case, with the healthy knee. Ask subcon when the knee can be fully healed. Leave the light there and future-pace say, three months and see the improvement, or go forward to the date by which it will be fully restored.

48. The decision is yours. The decision in this case was to charge half my normal fee, the second half to be paid when the client had benefited fully in health and lifestyle.

   A commitment in cash terms seems to be essential to success as part of the energy exchange. The debilitating influence of hand-outs becomes all too evident in 'welfare states'. Within a matter of weeks, in this case, the client had a remarkable stroke of good fortune. The balance of the fee was paid in three monthly instalments.

49. Normally five minutes. It can take an hour to vent fully.

50. Use a private therapy process and if necessary a silent abreaction. Only the client needs to know details of the problem to which a solution is required . . . to 'Problem X'. Work with feelings, again, without needing to have a description of the feelings involved.

51. By any dozens of indications, from initial eyelid flutter to imagining numbers on a ruler and, at the deeper levels, inability to respond to a direct instruction to raise an arm. If movement is required, the client must be returned to a lighter working level of relaxation.

52. The signalling finger tends to flutter rather than to rise stiffly. If there is any doubt, have the client try to raise the 'yes' finger consciously after putting it under subcon control. Ask subcon to

allow the thumbs to waggle if there is any conscious-mind interference, or have the cheeks blush . . . but only while working together as part of the healing process.

At an early stage, explain that you know that the client is becoming aware of the subconscious response actually before the fingers move and he can now provide the answers to your questions verbally.

When difficulty is experienced in establishing ideomotor responses, switch to another therapeutic process and return to ideodynamics later, if necessary switching and returning several times. It is also possible to establish effective signals by pretending, initially, that you are receiving acceptable signals.

53. In a moment you will return to full awakening consciousness knowing that you have been more deeply relaxed than ever before – more creatively relaxed – and this creative channel will always be available to you whenever it is appropriate for you to use it.

54. Great . . . so see yourself in a lift going up to the penthouse suite . . . notice how the floor numbers flicker by, one after the other . . . make the building as high as you like . . . and now the lift eases to a stop – the doors open – and you step out into a beautiful room – everything is just the way you choose it to be . . . and you look out on a wonderful view. It's a wonderful world and you know that everything worthwhile is achievable . . . and notice how deeply relaxed and at ease you feel . . . you are at home in this world.

55. Now in a moment I'm going to raise and drop one of your arms and the moment I do you will move to a good working level of creative relaxation and be able to respond clearly and correctly to each of my questions.

56. Have you been born yet?

57. Show the client's companion how to relax.

58. Now just sit with your hands placed comfortably on your lap and your feet placed firmly on the floor. (Avoid 'sit with your legs uncrossed').

59. Thank subcon and ask for the two-way communication channel to remain available for the benefit of the entire bodymind system, motivating the client to spontnaeous right action whenever required.

60. Guide the client to phase three relaxaton and say: 'I imagine you played dead many times as a child, so do that again and imagine this time that there is a difference . . . imagine that all the people you have known in your lifetime can gather around and talk about you and the first one to speak is your mother and she says . . . 'he was the most beautiful baby and I wanted him to enjoy every moment of his life' . . . what else would she say about you?'

61. You are both precisely on the same waveband.

62. You ensure, from the beginning, that your client is aware that your function is to show him how to maintain contact with the unlimited power and potential in himself . . . that he has the same power and potential, the same unlimited access to unlimited resources as anyone ever born to this planet. There are no exceptions. Nature doesn't play favourites. Why do we have to be shown? Because, from the start, we have accepted guidance from sometimes well-meaning but unmindful people. We have been manipulated or misled. Now you are learning a new form of dependence. You are learning to be dependent on yourself.

63. The major influences on your health and wellbeing are physical, mental, emotional, chemical and environmental. The keys to your problems are there to be found, deep in your own powerhouse mind.

64. It seems to provide a means of releasing to consciousness a new depth of understanding of emotional and other influences on personality and character formation. As with using the other ego or witness states to review a past event, it allows the client to stand back from an experience and gain perspective on some emotional influence on his present lifestyle.

Hints on Lüscher Testing

● The short-form, two-line/eight-colour Lüscher provides useful indications of stress intensity and personal problem areas to facilitate analysis and tape recommendations, indicating a client's reactions to current conditions and his/her general conditioning/personality traits.

● It helps to be able to convert the colours to numerals spontaneously (and *vice versa*), to know the significance of not only each colour but also of its order of choice and of any variations in the pattern of the first and second choice . . . and to be able to read stress intensity at a glance, for example: 3 2 0 1 4 5 6 7 . . . 7 6 5 0 1 2 3 4 . . . 6 2 3 1 0 4 5 7 translating to one, eleven and four. Stress two is the British average, three uncomfortable and anything over that, trouble.

● For many reasons, a two-line Lüscher is essential as an aid to effective analysis.

Compare:

(A)	4	3	7	0	6	1	2	5
	7	4	3	0	6	1	2	5
(B)	4	3	7	0	6	1	2	5
	7	4	0	6	3	1	2	5

(A) finds the existing situation disagreeable.
(B) is probably suicidal.

One or two sets of couplets 34/43, 12/21 etc. indicate a valid test. Absence of couplets indicates a confused person or an invalid test.

- Example of a test result:

```
   !!  !                    !!  !!!
   C  C  C           A  A  A
      x  x
   +  +  +  =  =  =  -  -  -
   4  6  7  0  1  5  2  3
   2  6  7  4  0  1  5  3
   +  +  +
      X  X  =  =  =  =
                     -  -  -
   C  C  C           A  A  A
   !!  !                 !    !!!
```

Heavy stress. No drive. . .no fight left in him/her. . .(–3). Pendulum swing from no resilience (–2) to over-assertiveness (+2) C.
(6) up front . . . sense of rootlessness. (=01) the Lüscher text just hints at what too often turns out to be a major problem indicator. These have included frustrated G-type personalities, sexual unorthodoxy/deviance, chronic weight problems, bulimia, concussion, leukemia, angina (concussion was later confirmed medically). (=10) is the same.
(+67)(x67) complete the sad picture.
Illness, over-tension or emotional distress have taken a severe toll, self-esteem reduced.
(+2) . . . hanging onto the ropes.
In several cases, (=01) or (=10), representing only stress level 2 at worst . . . has been the only indication of a serious underlying problem.

- The pattern 43 . . . 17 or 17 . . . 43 (and variations), not necessarily at the beginning and end of the eight colour choice . . . and not necessarily 'clear' . . . 453 . . . 71 for example, can indicate 'nerves' . . . the autonomic nervous system is upset . . . an indication of glandular problems, the thyroid the likely first target.
(The Pilgrim 'Study – Pass Exams' tape corrects this imbalance in students. 'Exam nerves' is a misnomer. Cramming for exams creates the mental/emotional imbalance long before the exam date. It surfaces in the exam-room atmosphere. A free pre-and post-exam Lüscher is provided to students who buy the tape . . . helping both the tapemaker and the student).

- Clients sometimes express the opinion that their choice of colours would be different each time. The second-line results of a test on an eight-year-old boy were as follows:

19/6/91   1 3 2 7 6 5 4 0
20/6/92   1 3 2 7 6 4 5 0

Tests have proved helpful in identifying the problem areas in children as young as three.

● It may be helpful to make a short note of the following points against the numbers in the Lüscher book. They are indicators only . . . they may not apply.
+13, 14 15 . . . can indicate that the client was a joyless only child . . . or a child born to a very young mother . . . an abused child . . . or a child born several years later than other brothers and sisters.

● Whenever 'unwilling to expose his/her vulnerability' appears in the text this can indicate G-type, sexual unorthodoxy or deviance . . . with demanding or manipulative personalities.

+26   Can indicate a serious problem . . . a 'terminal' anorexic, for example.

+45, 54, 50 Very immature, childish, G-type personality, victimised as a child.

+46, 62   Possibly concussed, punch-drunk.

+57   Strong emotional disappointment.

            Example:
                        1 3 5 7 6 0 2 4
                        5 7 1 3 0 2 6 4
            (a failed pop-star, aged 25).

x35   Childish, immature.

x41   Badly treated.

−01   Can be sexually unorthodox, the hormonal changes possibly initiated or stimulated by the use of 'blood-pressure' tablets.

−1   Frustrated G-type personality or concerned about homosexual tendencies.

−17   Strong sexual frustration, unorthodoxy or deviance.

−3   Dizziness under stress?

−30   Heart problem possibly.

−64   Can be serious . . . has shown with diabetes, heart problems, brain tumours, acute emotional problems.

+4–2   Aggressive AO-type.

+5–0   G-type.

+5–1   'Spiritually' conditioned, yoga type etc. Unable to accept responsibility or distinguish between fantasy and everyday living reality . . . can regress spontaneously to 'previous life experiences' as an evasive tactic. Requires skilful 'post-revelation' guidance to reawaken coping skills. Taped therapy is particularly useful here.

+51   **Sometimes** seen as a *compensation* when sexual inclinations are unorthodox. Up to teenage, is usually a reflection of immaturity, shyness, etc.

● The more competence you gain through interpreting test results and reading both selections to gauge where a minor increase in pressure (doing the test) reflects . . . the greater the benefit.

The following are selected from recent tests. For practice, you may wish to compare your findings with the brief case histories that follow the test results.

(A)   6 0 1 5 7 3 2 4
       0 6 3 1 7 5 2 4

(B)   1 5 3 4 2 0 6 7   (B) 3 4 1 5 2 0 7 6
       5 1 2 3 4 6 7 0   4 3 1 5 2 0 6 7

pre-therapy   post-therapy, age 24

(C)   4 1 5 2 0 3 6 7
       4 1 5 2 0 3 6 7

(D)   3 2 4 1 7 5 6 0
       4 2 1 3 0 7 6 5

(E)   3 7 2 5 4 1 0 6
       4 7 5 3 1 0 6 2

(F)   2 4 3 5 6 1 7 0
       2 3 5 6 4 1 0 7

(G) 4 2 3 0 5 6 7 1   (G) 2 0 4 1 5 6 3 7
     4 3 6 5 2 7 0 1   1 5 2 0 4 6 7 3
                (9 am)   (7 pm)
            Both before therapy
(H) 2 3 4 5 1 6 7 0
     3 4 2 5 1 7 6 0
(I) 3 2 4 5 1 0 7 6
     2 3 4 5 1 0 6 7

(A) *Lady, executive, 45, recently lost her job, her husband, her home. Threatened with a sixth breast cancer operation. Apart from the high stress level, 06 and 24 are indicative. (Foundling child, three serious car accidents and one hit-and-run. Health now OK, lifestyle dramatically improved. The bigger the log-jam, the faster it breaks).*

(B) *Teenager – aggressively jealous (due to fear of abandonment). Brilliant imagination . . . spontaneous 'past life regression'. Second (and final) session cleared the screening/reality-evading process to: 3 4 1 5 2 0 7 6 . . . 4 3 1 5 2 0 6 7.*

(C) *Age 41. Badly treated by parents and partner.*

(D) *Sublimated artistic sensitivity . . . (–65). Attractive psychology graduate. Therapy to overcome difficulty in making presentations and to avoid failing in a training course organised by a large drug company, focused on introducing three new drugs to medical practitioners.*

(E) *(Same week). Senior medical research chemist, under constant pressure to achieve results to justify high research expenditure. Stress further aggravated by his awareness of the disparity between his professional reports and the eventual marketing publicity.*

(F) *A declared 'terminal' cancer client, since fully 'cleared'. Indications are that a person has fully accepted the authoritative negative conditioning if 2, 3 and 4 are in the last four or five places. In this event, I personally insist on seeing a positive response to my cancer relief tapes before accepting a client for one-session precision therapy, to ensure that the results are rewarding to both parties.*

(G) *The lady client proudly presented me with two test results chosen by her on the same day. Next question? 'Have you had psychiatric help at any time?' She cheerily announced that she had been receiving treatment as a schizophrenic for twenty years. Resolving her problems required six hours' therapy in two sessions. A benevolent alter-ego had become dissociated when the girl was sexually molested by a relative at the age of two.*

(H) and (I) are typical 'carer' profiles. An October 1989 diary entry reads:

> *Dream Stuff* This one had 3 miles, 4 minutes and 25 pesetas in it . . . Lüscher! +34 and x25 rang a bell. Looked it up. Fellow analyst's results of yesterday, 2nd line 3 4 2 5 1 0 7 6, so what? Hold on . . . nursing sister 5 2 3 4 / 1 6 7 0, radiologist, 5 2 4 3 / 1 0 7 6. Check back . . . social service, masseur, nurse, rebirther, all this 2 3 4 5 / 1 0 7 6 type split. **And this chap in a bookshop in London** who sells my tapes . . . why him? Asked. Leading NLP therapist.

Note the (=10) in the (I) selection. (The nursing sister involved confirmed she had experienced angina attacks). The 'carer' pattern indicates breadth of feeling rather than depth of regard for any one person. The nearer the 5 to the first choice, the greater the emotional sensitivity, vulnerability and immaturity . . . the less effective the therapist.

When 5 is chosen last, the client can be cut off from imagination or sealed against help with conscious self-hypnosis.

In career and management consultancy particularly, a useful comparison can be made between the client's job needs (x) and the objective and means of achieving them (+).

There is no perfect score in the Lüscher test . . . Dr Max Lüscher recognising that perfection is not a human attribute. We can attain to excellence from time to time. A top-dog therapist would probably produce something like (43) (21) (56) (07). A top business executive (3) (42) (15) (60) (7).

A good number two (42) (31) (56) (07).

As an analyst you can learn to appreciate that honesty, like charity, must start at home so that, even after years of functional psychology tests, you can still find the Lüscher useful for yourself.

Analytical Tape /Script 'NRG+' (Pilgrim)

This tape is featured only on the professional list and is available to therapists for professional use. It can also be issued to tape or therapy clients whose stress levels are below three on the Lüscher scale. This is side 'A' . . . a sit-to tape. It can be slept-to when repressed emotions are satisfactorily released. Side 'B' is an energy-stimulating subliminal.

Hello . . . greetings . . . and welcome . . .

Your life can be fun. Every phase of your life can be a joy . . . and of course, it all now depends on you . . . because you . . . and only you, can allow thoughts to live in your mind . . . and how you think determines how you feel . . . and how you feel influences the world around you . . . and you can learn how to choose your thoughts with awareness of their power . . . you can seed beneficial thoughts in your mind and from the very first occasion on which you play this tape, a simple process of putting you fully in charge of your thoughts will be set in motion . . . and day by day, you'll find more and more, how important it is to choose your every thought with care . . . because the thoughts you seed in your mind . . . the concepts and beliefs you accept with feeling, inevitably become your own living reality. How you choose to think today influences all your tomorrows . . . and your life is too valuable . . . too miraculous . . . to be left to chance . . . to be allowed to become a shabby, second-rate, carbon copy of somebody else's . . . for this planet is a gameplayer's planet . . . and the big game in life is a kind of treasurehunt with the real you as the hidden treasure . . . and the real you is a treasure worth finding . . . for, for you, there's no greater treasure on earth. And it's an easy game . . . because life is meant to be easy . . . in fact . . . you can find your way to the treasurehouse within while you relax . . . and even while you sleep.

And to make these assurances your everyday living reality . . . I invite you now to relax . . . to relax and make yourself as comfortable

161

as possible . . . and if it's your bedtime, that's great . . . or perhaps you prefer to sit with your back well supported, with both feet placed firmly on the floor . . . and with your hands resting comfortably on your lap.

Now, allow your eyes to close, normally and naturally, as you begin by gently drawing in a long, slow, deep breath by way of the nose . . . hold the breath for the mental count of four . . . and now slightly open the mouth as you release all the air from the body in a long, low, deep sigh . . . and relax. Just release, relax and let go . . . let go now . . . as I guide you by the scenic route on a journey of self-discovery. Near the end of the recording, awakening signals are given which your subconscious control mind will only ignore if you're choosing to play this tape at your bedtime . . . in this event you'll shortly find yourself drifting off into a refreshingly natural sleep . . . and this will be entirely beneficial – because positive recommendations for behavioural change will be directly received, understood and implemented by the subconscious control levels of mind, to the precise degree that they're appropriate to ensuring your vibrant good health and physical, mental and emotional harmony and balance.

And day by day, as your self-understanding continues to develop and expand, the quality of your self-understanding becomes the measure of your personal power . . . your power to grow, to mature, to help and to heal . . . so, this time, double your state of relaxation as you allow your stomach to relax and expand . . . and gently draw in another long, slow, deep breath . . . hold . . . hold . . . now, slowly release all the air from the body as I count . . . 8 . . . 7 . . . 6 . . . 5 . . . 4 . . . 3 . . . 2 . . . 1 . . . zero . . . zero . . . zero . . . and relax . . . just release, relax and let go . . . let go all the cares . . . and the worries, all the tensions and pressures and stresses and strains . . . let them all ease from the body and release from the mind . . . and allow yourself to drift down . . . down . . . down . . . into a deeper, to a more blissful state of creative relaxation . . . for the deeper you go . . . the better you feel . . . and the better you feel, the deeper you go . . . peace, serenity, just letting go . . . centred, relaxed, still more fully in control.

Now – as a progressive relaxation programme will shortly be provided, I know you'll appreciate that this recording should never be played beyond this point while driving, or at any other time, for that matter, when your full attention may be otherwise required . . .

. . . also know that at any time, while practising self-hynosis, either alone or with the aid of a recording such as this, you can immediately return to full awakening consciousness merely by counting the numbers from one to five either mentally or out loud . . . and should a need arise while practising self-hypnosis, you will immediately return to full awakening consciousness and whatever the need, you will handle it in a cool, calm and highly competent manner.

Now, in your mind . . . in your creative imagination, reach up and bring the sunlight down. Bring the sunlight down to form a brilliant ball of golden light-energy all around you . . . a force-field of positive healing energy if you like . . . and feel and know . . . and experience that, at the count of three, you are fully protected from all self-limiting negative emanations from whatever source . . . now – and for the next twenty-four hours . . . 1 . . . 2 . . . 3 . . . and inhale – deeply inhale Lifeforce . . . and as you sleep or relax still more deeply, bring the healing-power of mental sunlight into your heart by way of the head . . . and feel, and experience it there, radiating, radiating, pulsating, vibrating throughout the entire blood-stream and out to every nerve and cell and system of the body . . . and as the light moves, the light glows . . . and warms . . . and soothes . . . and heals . . . and you release . . . and relax . . . and drift down, down, down, deeper and deeper into relaxation. Now . . . leave the light there. The light knows what to do. The bodymind system knows how to respond. Just relax . . . and move more and more into harmony with Lifeforce . . . into tune with the one universal life-flow.

The major influences on our health and wellbeing are recognised as being physical, mental, emotional, chemical and thermal. Situation and psyche and parental neuroses all play their part . . . so that your problems may not all seem to be all in your mind . . . but the solution to all your problems is always there to be found . . . deep – deep in your own powerhouse mind. So once again, call on the creative power of your imagination and see rising up and all around you, outlining every contour of your body, a brilliant, violet flame . . . a purifying flame . . . that ancient, noble flame that preceded light . . . long recognised by the human mind as symbolising the positive transmuting power of the deepest possible form of human understanding – which is love . . . and affirm . . . at the count of three, all self-limiting negative influences in, on and all around me are transmuted to strong, positive, constructive, creative and life-sustaining influences, acting in, on and all around me now . . . and for the next twenty-four hours . . . 1 . . . 2 . . . 3 . . . and again inhale . . . deeply inhale Lifeforce and feel and know and experience that the mental cleansing process has been effectively accomplished. Self-limiting doubts and other negative influences may arise from time to time, but you will cease to entertain them. You will cancel them, right in the moment, by mentally repeating 'cancel, cancel' and the learning experience or creative opportunities that the nega- tivity has sought to conceal, will be revealed to you . . . opportunities to increase your self-unerstanding . . . your understanding of others . . . your understanding of life.

You'll be motivated to play this recording often . . . and whenever you focus on your breathing pattern and mentally repeat . . . 1 . . . 2 . . . 3 . . . relax, relax, or whenever the word relax is used in this recording, all unnecessary movements of the body and distractive activities of the mind will cease . . . and a deep sense of peace and harmony will permeate your personal universe, your bodymind system, as you become still more creatively relaxed and at ease . . . more at ease with the world . . . more at ease with yourself . . . more at ease with everyone. And now – call once more on the positive transmuting power of the violet flame, as you affirm with me at the count of three, all self-limiting bonds with people and events and experiences of the past are now severed and released forever . . . in the light of true understanding. All those who have offended me, I forgive, as I am forgiven by all those whom I have offended . . . and most of all, I forgive myself for unwittingly setting all these things in motion . . . 1 . . . 2 . . . 3 . . . and inhale – deeply inhale Lifeforce. You relax and forgive – you live – and let live . . . and daily you relax and send the mental sunlight ahead of you . . . to wherever your journeys lead . . . to your home . . . and to all the people in your life, one by one. They will benefit and so will you, for the more light you send in your thoughts to others, the more light, you will find, will reflect back on you.

Each and every time you relax to this recording, your understand- ing of the degree to which each and every one of us has been negatively conditioned will be further increased . . . and whatever self-limiting negative myths, beliefs and impressions that you have unwittingly absorbed in the past – will be released, one by one, through the natural medium of dreams and experiences at a rate consistent with maintaining your vibrant good health and mental, physical and emotional wellbeing . . . and you will automatically be stimulated to develop beneficial behavioural patterns to replace the inhibitory ones, so that, day by day, you will increasingly unify and focus the full creative power and potential of your mind in achiev- ing whatever worthwhile aims and objectives you have in mind.

Now . . . as you relax, focus your feelings, from within, on your lips. Be aware of the sensitivity of your lips and feel the tender tissue tingle as you focus more thought-energy there. And now, still focus- ing on feeling, gently raise the corners of your lips in a tiny smile . . .

and feel the smile spreading to relax the tiny muscles around the eyes, as your finer senses respond to the subtle message of the smile . . . relaxing the brain . . . such a tiny thing . . . such a powerful influence . . .influencing so many internal functions – even changing your feelings about the world around you, for as you relax and smile, you bring more sunlight into life . . . into your life, and into the lives of others . . . for there is magic . . . powerful magic in your smile.

And now, still maintaining the smile, focus your mindpower on your tongue . . . on the sensitivity of your tongue . . . and as excess saliva forms in the mouth, just swallow it – swallow it and go down, down, down, still more deeply into relaxation . . . for the simple fact is that, through the subtle, psychodynamic processes of the mind, you have both the power and the potential to monitor and direct your thought energies . . . to modify the vibrational levels in **any** area of your body . . . and influence all those physical aspects of your being that you've been misled into thinking are outside your conscious levels of understanding and control. Only your own, linear-conditioned, chatterbox mind has ever stood in your way. Using conscious instead of unconscious self-hypnosis, you cease to be distracted from constructive, creative and life-sustaining purpose.

Now . . . to improve the quality of your awareness, and to deepen your powers of concentration, so that you can always focus your mindpower on whatever you choose to select and eliminate all disruptive, distractive and other useless thought-forms at will, tune in to those parts of the body that you feel are most comfortable and allow the feeling of comfort to deepen and spread throughout the rest of the body, all the way down to your toes.

And soon – soon I'll be asking the subconscious control levels of mind, on your behalf, to coordinate all bodymind functions in dealing with whatever symptom, problem or issue you want to relieve or resolve – some problem that perhaps owes its origin to an experience or an event in the past that has moved outside your conscious recollection and control but persists, below the level of consciousness, in disrupting the natural process of regulation and control in some part, or parts, or functions of the bodymind system. As you relax, in that passive centre of creative calm and control you've rediscovered in your mind, you provide the climate for change. You allow the unlimited power and potential of your own creative mind to come more fully into play. You move, more and more, into harmony and balance with Lifeforce, with all those subtle and all-pervasive life energies, in, on and all around you that energise and animate every living cell and atom. You gain access to your unlimited personal potential. You move to a more elevated mental vantage point in life and your powers of creative insight and intuition will automatically develop and expand. Just want it to happen – know it can happen – it happens . . . for your personal benefit – and for the benefit of all. As another part of our unnatural conditioning – as part of the social charade, we've been persuaded since birth to be active – to be doing something most, if not all of the time – to accept as normal, a constant mental condition of restlessness – of fight or flight, burying our real feelings, our emotions, deep inside . . . deep inside, where our vital organs are overburdened with keeping the score.

Your inner guardian – your subconscious control mind, is the regulator of all your biological and mental processes . . . and every single incident in your life is graphically recorded and firmly imprinted at the deeper levels of awareness, in your unique, psychobiological consciousness. Centred, relaxed and more deeply aware, you can return to any event instantly, to see the event unfold as a witness, not as a function of memory (because memory is always faulty, memory always reconstructs) – but to see the event as it actually happened, happening again . . . and releasing any errors of thought and self-limiting negative emotions that the more mature adult consciousness can now put into true perspective and release from the psyche forever, freeing the bodymind system for more creative purpose in life. So – choose a problem you have. Select any sense of limitation or lack or need and bring it clearly to mind. Do that now . . . or allow subcon to choose . . . and now – inhale . . . deeply inhale Lifeforce . . . bring on the unwelcome feelings as I ask the control levels of mind, on your behalf, and for the benefit of the entire bodymind system, to re-open two-way communication between all levels of mind, as you drift back in time . . . back in time to just before the initial sensitising event – to just before the first occasion on which the problem you've chosen arose. Going back to just before the causal factor. Back now at the count of three. Back, as the event begins to unfold . . . 1 . . . 2 . . . 3 . . . (*) . . . now witness the event . . . see it unfold, from beginning to end as you modify or expand on the questions I now ask on your behalf.

Where are you now – indoors or outdoors? Is it night or day? Are you alone or with someone? How old are you? And what's happening? What are you doing? The person or people with you – what are they saying or doing? Clarify the picture (*). What is being said or done to shock/hurt/frighten/offend or annoy you? Self-doubt, anger, frustration, confusion – what are your emotions? The sense of insecurity, inadequacy or lack – what is causing it to arise? . . . Who did you decide to blame? Get fully in touch with any feelings of discomfort, resentment, guilt or shame . . . What have you learned from the experience? What have you learned from the experience that will be useful – useful to you now . . . and again and again? You can see it now . . . is there any earlier event that helped to create the problem? You'll see the event. Are there any later events, in which the same pattern arose . . . link and connect the feelings . . .

And now – now let it all go. Shed the anger . . . the fear . . . the frustration . . . the pain. All the emotions too heavy to bear at the time – let them go. There's no-one to blame. At the count of three, let them all go and be free . . . 1 . . . 2 . . . 3 . . . (*).

And come back now. Come back now to the present . . . to this ever-new moment of now.

The misunderstandings and other errors of thought, the lack of sensitivity and foresight and whatever other influences helped create your problems in the past, will be released to consciousness one by one and will lose their negative hold on you whenever your consciousness is ready to deal with them effectively . . . and whenever you return to this recording, your ability to access the deeper levels of self-understanding will grow and grow . . . and you'll be completely free from the self-limiting negative influences of all those dreary dramas of dead yesterdays . . . always releasing repressed emotions at a rate and intensity consistent with maintaining full physical, mental and emotional harmony and balance. You'll be free from the past – and the past will be free from you . . . and your entire bodymind system will celebrate . . . it will rejoice . . .

And now – mentally thank the subconscious control mind for guiding you patiently to the path of deeper self-understanding . . . that insistent voice – inside – that the superficial, conditioned levels of mind, have tried for so long and so often, to ignore . . . and feel and know and experience that all the orderly modifications, adjustments and improvements, essential to your health, success and happiness, are already taking place – and even while you sleep. For the aim of the subconscious control mind is always lifewards and nature is forever seeking new channels for creative expression . . . centred and relaxed, you provide such a channel.

The thinking mind is mind in motion – a guessing mind. Lost in your thoughts, you fail to come to your senses . . . to those vital senses that moment to moment keep you youthful, happy, healthy, responsive, alert and alive. All knowing and power comes from the stillness, from that passive centre of creative calm and control in your being . . . for this – this is your channel to Lifeforce . . . so relax

. . . centre . . . go to where the power is . . . and you will be helped . . . and you will be healed.

You may, of course, wonder how the subconscious control mind can so easily arrange for you to achieve whatever objectives you have in mind, once you detach your thoughts from your problems and make a firm decision about the direction in which you want to go, and this is understandable because each and every one of us has a vast sphere of identity – a force-field of creative mindpower that we have been conditioned by fear and ignorance to fail to explore . . . a veritable treasurehouse of health-intelligence and life-understanding. This incredibly elevated level of mindpower responsible, amongst millions of other functions, for ensuring that over 100,000 discreet chemical changes are made in the body every single second . . . for accelerating 25 billion blood cells around the entire bodymind system every 15 seconds of your life, in an incredible all-stations-renovation-and-rejuvenation service . . .

. . . for directing 400 million cells to separate oxygen from every breath that you take, and for making available 14 billion possible neural responses . . . over 1,000 times more connections than the world's entire network of telephone services. And this . . . this incredible mindpower, this personal treasurehouse . . . this is the area of mindpower we have been carefully conditioned by misguided, manipulative or unmindful men, throughout the history of mankind, to fail to explore.

The way this life-sustaining mind works is governed by strict universal laws, including the universal law of attraction, for, whenever you allow your conscious mind to become focused on your problems, you drag your problems into the future with you, and they automatically attract still more of the same. Your ill-fortune becomes as much an outgrowth from you as your own arms and legs. Your own negative thought-patterns provide the psychic energies that feed your problems and keep them alive. So just relax and switch the polarity around and focus your thought energy on how you *want things to be, rather than how you don't want them to be* . . . and withdraw all your thought energy from the problems, so that you attract the solutions . . . you attract good fortune like a magnet. The control mind now knows what you want, and what you want, or something even more useful, presents itself, as though what you have been always seeking has, somehow, always been seeking you . . . seeking to find creative expression in your everyday living reality . . . and the incredible fact is . . . that it has.

So – if you have a habit, or a behavioural pattern that you intend to change, firstly . . . bring it to mind. Become conscious that something that is not as you desire it to be is attracting enough energy from you to enable it to persist in your life despite your desire to eliminate it. Bring this habit or limitation to mind at the count of three. It may be some capability that you wish to improve, or perhaps you want to cease responding in anger or being too easily distracted from the job in hand . . . so . . . choose the pattern you want to change or the skill or capability you want to improve at the count of three. What you want to modify, change or improve . . . 1 . . . 2 . . . 3 . . . Again, at the count of three, go back to an event or an occasion in which the maladaptive habit or response or the desire to perform better occurred . . . and see what triggered your reaction or caused you to respond in some way other than the way you'd like to respond. Go through the thought-patterns that precede the event . . . bring to mind the actions you take and the emotions you feel as the event or experience begins to unfold . . . the sights, the sounds . . . the feelings involved. Be aware of what you do just before the unwelcome state of being occurs . . . and be aware of how really undesirable it is . . . link the feeling to the event. At the count of three . . . 1 . . . 2 . . . 3 . . . see the event clearly . . . make the mental picture big and bright . . . illuminate every aspect of it . . . make it clear . . . bring the picture up close . . . let it fill the screen of the mind . . . you want to know all about it . . .

Make it a moving picture if you like . . . it's big and it's bright – and it's not what you want. Now . . . create a new picture . . . a small picture . . . a picture of you as you see yourself having accomplished the desired change. The unwanted pattern of behaviour has ceased. Everything is exactly as you want it to be . . . see it . . . feel it . . . know it . . . experience it . . . see the picture, still overshadowed by the unwanted picture – perhaps a little indistinct . . . it's small, it's unclear. Now, at the count of three, switch the polarity . . . switch the pictures. See the unwanted picture darken, diminish, go out of focus . . . see it spinning off into the distance . . . see it disappear . . . 1 . . . 2 . . . 3 . . . and see the new picture brighten . . . everything just as you want it to be . . . the picture becoming clearer, brighter, bigger. The new picture dominates the screen . . . brilliant, beautiful, *wonderful.* And leave the picture in the mirror of the mind to serve as an attracting force – and it will! Just want it to happen, know it can happen – it happens. You struggled with your problems in the past and tried to outrun the shadow of your past conditioning . . . now you can relax . . . just relax and create the attracting force from the stillness . . . and be amazed at the quality of the success that you attract. Your creative mind ensures only right action . . . spontaneous right action . . . and only right action prospers all. Self-doubt and repressed emotions created most, if not all, of our problems and pains in life. Self-understanding and emotion provide the channel for release . . . so relax still deeper as I guide you now on another journey. On a gentle journey. On a journey into your past.

On a journey you are perhaps intended to make, perhaps even expected to make as a child of the Universe . . . as an infant child of the Universe . . . and you may wish to choose this journey as your own . . . for this journey will set you free . . . free from all the hurts and illusions of the past. Whatever self-limiting illusions you may have unwittingly accepted in the past, will now be replaced by creative self-understanding – understanding that your entire being will celebrate . . . for you were educated away from your nature and from your natural good health. Now – you find your way back. As you relax, imagine yourself becoming younger again . . . younger and smaller . . . smaller and smaller . . . your legs growing shorter . . . your arms growing shorter. Your body becoming smaller and smaller . . . younger and smaller . . . until now you know yourself once again as an infant child . . . a healthy, happy infant child . . . nurtured, comforted, supported and sustained, as you go back in time – in imagination – to infancy, see yourself now as that tiny child as you mentally rewrite your personal history, making whatever changes to the past that you want . . . move in closely . . . move in closer now to you – the infant child – and tell me what you see. Tell me what you want to see . . . because your life is your personal choice, now and always. So choose . . . choose this time with care . . . with care and deep understanding . . . choose now . . . and look deeply into the wondering eyes of the tiny child . . . what do you see? Love . . . deep, deep love of life and everything in it . . . so much love to offer. So much love to share.

A human . . . being. Not a human . . . thinking, doubting, worrying. The tiny child still lives within you now . . . still reaching out with love to give . . . with love to share . . . so allow this younger part of you to live – to live again – to live . . . your dream, your choice in life. Through your infant eyes, see your mother, a human . . . being. Not a human . . . thinking, doubting, worrying. And see your father, a human . . . being. Not a human . . . thinking, doubting, worrying. So much love to give, so much love to share. Explaining, guiding, encouraging you, encouraging you as a child to find expression for your developing skills and talents. Understanding you . . . encouraging you as day by day your needs change . . . as day by day you increase your understanding together. With understanding, you find no need for orders or punishment or guilt or blame or shame. Just fresh choices – new opportunities . . .

easily recognised, clarified, explained. Experiencing the joy of discovery in this magical world . . . aware of the needs of the body and the needs of the mind. Finding time for understanding . . . finding time for love – a true child of the Universe, enjoying the splendour of being, celebrating just being, being loved, and loving just being alive.

Come back . . . come back to now. Back to yourself, back to the present, back to this ever-new moment of now and bring this history into being as part of your own living reality, as whatever reality you choose it to be . . . as a child of the Universe, a child of light and life – and love . . . you are free.

And this . . . this is the fresh pattern your subconscious control mind will now carry forward from your childhood to your adult life. Free from the problems and self-limiting influences that only arose through misunderstandings and false beliefs. You're entering a new world of experience, a new quality of life . . . a more elevated mental and emotional vantage point from which the best options and opportunities in life are always available . . . will always be seen. For the fact is, that you're both the magician and the beneficiary of your own magic and now you choose for your magic in life – Lifeforce . . . love, life, light, health, wealth and happiness, and success and fulfilment in all things. Stay with the magic . . . the magic of mindpower . . . the magic will stay with you!

You now rule over your personal universe – your bodymind system – with love and respect, for it's by far the greatest gift you may ever receive, and your eating, drinking, sleeping and other living habits are now all consistent with maintaining your vibrant good health and abundant creative energy. The immune system and all other systems, nerves, cells and functions of the body are performing normally and the basal metabolism rate is adjusted as necessary to maintain the body in its ideal condition, weight, shape and form. Each night, you release the day, in the sure and certain understanding that the orderly modifications, adjustments and restorations that are appropriate to ensuring your health and happiness are already taking place . . . and you will greet each new day with a healthy body and with an alert, responsive and creative mind.

You now find that you can respond to others in ways that are worthy of you – whether or not they are worthy of them, for you now radiate self-confidence and understanding of life. The way you walk and talk and dress and behave reflects your deep sense of personal self-worth and self-respect . . . and every day you just look and feel better and better, for you know that there are no limitations to your success and enjoyment in life . . . other than those that you unwittingly imposed on yourself in the past.

And now you know the pathway to the vast treasurehouse within . . . and all the power and potential, and all the love and joy and inspiration you'll ever need in life is there – in your own powerhouse mind. And to call on the unlimited power and potential of your own very best friend, your infallible inner guide or guardian, you just deeply inhale, deeply inhale Lifeforce and go to where the true power is . . . as a true child of the Universe, as a child of light, of life, of love. And this Universe will celebrate. This Universe will rejoice. And daily, you find more opportunities to invest more time in self-understanding . . . and like the impeccable hunter, you make your weaknesses your prey and hunt them down, one by one, submitting them to the light of understanding against which all forms of self-limiting negativity must yield. And mentally, affirm this deeper understanding . . . and in affirming, the focusing power of your own creative mind makes it real. As I mentally relax, I deeply inhale . . . I **deeply** inhale Lifeforce.

Feeling so good, responsive, aware . . . comforted, secure . . . at ease with myself, at ease with the world . . . at ease with everyone . . . for I am all the joy and the love and the bliss in life in the fullness of expression. I am comforted, protected, supported and sustained, moving with ease through time and space, guided always by the light and the life and the love within me. As a child of the Universe, I flow with the river of life through this wonderful world of experience, this constant miracle of everyday living reality . . . born to live . . . to laugh . . . to love . . . to learn . . . every new moment of now. Peace and peace and peace to everyone. Love and life and light to all. And now smile, fellow pilgrim, smile . . . and bring more sunshine into life . . .

Now, in a moment, you'll be conscious of hearing the wake-up signal . . . the count-up from one to five and if this is your normal bed-time, you'll ignore the wake-up signal completely and continue sleeping blissfully until your desired awakening time, when you will awaken feeling fully refreshed and rejuvenated and eager to greet another great new day. However, if this is other than your normal bed-time, you will awaken at the count of five. At the count of five, your eyes will open and you'll become fully alert, with energy flowing through your body and with healthy and harmonious thoughts in your mind.

And the count is one . . . beginning to respond . . . two . . . coming up . . . three . . . moving, stretching . . . four . . . if this *is* your normal bedtime sleep on in the sure and certain understanding that a great

new world of opportunity always awaits your awakening and five
. . . the number 'five' has been called, and if this is other than your
normal bedtime, your eyes are now open and you are now fully
awake . . . fully awake to your incredibly creative powers of mind
and to your positively unlimited personal potential.

Therapy Tapes

An advantage in providing prospective clients with a short cassette tape describing your services is that the client's friends and family, as well as the client, can at least shed some of their misconceptions. Including a short, effective relaxation induction of the kind featured in the Pilgrim 'Rapid Relaxation' tape can be useful. Depending upon the nature of the client's problems, other tapes on specific subjects can help to save time and expense and ensure effective therapy.

Whatever the recording, be sure to include a suggestion to subcon, whether you think that it is necessary or not, to implement the affirmations only to the extent that they are beneficial in attaining or maintaining harmony and balance throughout the entire bodymind system.

To avoid any possibility of 'attachment' or the need to go to the ridiculous extreme of asking for the tape to be returned, some variation of the following stock phrase can be included in the narrative, to supplement the earlier suggestion to subcon control:

> 'All beliefs, spiritual, esoteric or otherwise, are obstacles – they become barriers to deeper understanding. When you find a source of understanding such as this tape, accept, be grateful and then move on . . . move on to greater things.'

The following information is provided in the current Pilgrim Tapes professional release.

PILGRIM TAPES PROFESSIONAL RELEASE

Audio cassette tapes uniquely designed to facilitate the analytical process and extend the healing process beyond the 'once-a-weekly'. The information is provided to inform rather than to promote.

STRESS

Social Services are amongst those who have used this tape to relieve stressed clients . . . including manic depressives and incipient suicides. The tape also facilitates therapy by reducing high stress levels and restoring self-confidence. For clients in areas in which I have been unable to recommend a therapist personally, the stress tape alone has reduced stress levels from eight to one on the Lüscher scale.

CANCEL CANCER

The officially recognised score for spontaneous remissions is one in twenty thousand. Clients who decide to 'try' hypnotherapy are not your average citizens. They have overcome their unreasoned fears of hypnosis, and they entertain hope, that essential ingredient in healing that it is unlawful to offer anyone in writing.

My initial practice was to issue this tape to clients, requiring payment when full remission had been confirmed. Over eighty percent of clients paid within twelve weeks, many in eight.

Leading specialists in the UK, USA, Germany and Mexico have contributed greatly to the recordings.

The original tape has been updated seven times since 1987 as experience in one-session therapy revealed more effective ways of dealing with the various manifestations of cancer. A strong double-subliminal version is now available and CC2 evolved in 1992 . . . designed to deal with the causal and compounding factors. It has been used effectively by clients aged ten to seventy who had responded to 'CC1' and 'CC subliminal' and whose stress levels on the Lüscher scale were below four.

A feature of these tapes is that anyone hearing them experiences a noticeable energy boost as the innate fear we all inherit, even of the word 'cancer', is eliminated once and for all.

Clients who have benefited personally from using the 'CC' tapes over the last five years are happy to tell their success stories.

SERENITY (Enhanced coping skills)

Anyone who has experienced an unhealthy or maladaptive form of existence for several years and is now aware of the causal factors may have exceptional needs for guidance and reassurance, particularly when their environment remains unchanged. This double subliminal tape reinforces whatever ego-boosting suggestions one can devise in an unusually effective way. The beneficial influence is apparent immediately. It endures.

SUCCESS

As the client attains that blissful state of release from his problems . . . what about the transitional period as he applies his newfound perspective to his old environment? The 'Success' tape can work wonders here. In fact, an interesting book could be written about the successes achieved with this tape alone. The creative series and 'NRG+' then provide entry to the major league.

NRG+

This tape is unlisted. It is for issue exclusively to and by therapists. Hearing side 'A', you will appreciate how and why it stimulates daily insights.

The subliminal on side 'B' evolved from a one-off tape prepared to meet an exceptional need, a medical request that triggered a breakthrough in subliminal therapy that astounded me as much as the hospital staff involved. Biomonitoring and field reports from UK and USA therapists confirm that the subliminal influence provides a strong and enduring energy boost.

LOVE AWARENESS

A useful self-understanding tape and also one for the 80% or more Britons who are emotionally inhibited.

PAIN RELIEF

Natural conscious hypnosis techniques are conveyed to stimulate specific neurotransmitters to discontinue pain signals and activate endorphins and enkephalins, the body's own intelligent painkilling cells, without mind-dulling and other negative side effects. The pain suppression influence is calculated to be at least two hundred times more effective than morphine. To meet all needs, the pain removal suggestions are only made effective for periods of 24 hours, renewable as required.

CREATIVE DREAMPOWER

'Horses for courses' always applies, but I have yet to hear from anyone who has failed to benefit in practical terms from this gestalt-inspired approach to dream understanding. Useful for the therapist and for the exceptional analysand. The solutions to all our problems are nightly on tap.

MENOPAUSE & PMT/PMS RELIEF

NLP, analysis and other techniques are provided in both these tapes to overcome the maladaptive conditioning (the usual social stresses compounded by parental and other forms of insensitivity and bodymind ignorance) that allow less than 20% of women to experience natural and comfortable transitions in their vital reproductive faculties.

UNDERSTANDING PARENTS

Originally intended to relieve children of divorced parents from their inevitably false sense of personal guilt (feeling they had caused the problem), the tape has proved successful in resolving a wide range of serious problems in children of all ages . . . well, from 4 months to 74 years so far.

Recommended for whenever parental insensitivity or worse may have been a factor in contributing to current problems.

CHAKRA MEDITATION

A special request tape that I treated as a cosmetic until I awakened to the scope it provided for combining 100% positive suggestions with techniques for getting clients more in touch with their internal resources. Confused teenagers, jaded analysts and hard-nosed business executives are amongst those who have benefited from taking the occasional journey by the scenic route around the seven energy centres in the body. After thousands of years of disbelief the scientific community can now confirm that these vital intelligent energy centres actually exist.

FERTILITY

Perhaps because hypnotherapy is often seen as a last resort, this tape has produced the desired results within three months when treatments costing £3,000 to £12,000 have proved ineffective. Another possible explanation, in several cases, is that the medical tests were faulty, as Lüscher tests indicated that the husband was vulnerable to a serious health problem. The tape is usually heard by both partners.

GENTLE CHILDBIRTH

The double-subliminal tape evolved in a matter of hours to meet an exceptional need. Linked with 'Happy Childbirth' and 'Rapid Relaxation', it is still producing results that add to my cheery collection of baby photographs.

WHISPER SUBLIMINALS – PILGRIM ORIGINAL

A medical request in 1992 for a tape to be played in a general ward to help patients who had not been advised of the terminal nature of their problems was met by providing a subliminal tape with a difference . . . well, two differences. The volume of the accelerated subliminal message was reduced to a whisper so that it could be made inaudible when played and the message was not masked by music. The beneficial results were unusually impressive and have since been confirmed by providing whisper subliminals for subjects ranging from asthma to excema . . . and cancer elimination. Whisper subliminals can be played at any time, including while the client is viewing television.

PAST-LIFE EXPERIENCES

A basic theme in analysis is to stimulate clients to find out the truth in themselves. Screen memory and cryptoamnesia concepts apart, the therapeutic influence of past-life experiences, imagined or real, has been found by many world-renowned authors and therapists to stimulate self-understanding and the release of consciously-repressed material, without unpleasant emotional reactions. The tape achieves this.

TRUST TAPE

A double-sided C90 subliminal designed to assist in all stages of effective analysis. The script is provided. Biomonitoring confirms that the abreactive influence bypasses the therapist and is correctly channelled to the client, consequently no special audio equipment is required and the tape can be played continuously.

SPECIAL TAPES

A selection of special-purpose tapes is available covering various aspects of therapy and dealing subliminally with the type of problems that otherwise require the establishment of an unusually high degree of empathy. The subliminal techniques used throughout are based on those recommended by the leading USA researchers on subliminal persuasion including one for whom I worked who has sold more than five million health tapes worldwide.

Aversion techniques are excluded from all Pilgrim Tapes, as

aversion is clearly as unbalanced a state of mind as addiction and no therapist worthy of the title would induce negative conditioning.

Assistance and advice on preparing subliminal scripts is offered free of charge to fellow therapists.

Special subliminals include (medical) coma release and dealing with all forms of eye problems, cold extremities, flashing, sexual irregularities, breast development, autism, dyslexia, dispersal of cysts, strokes/paralysis and unusual compulsions and phobic reactions.

THERAPY TAPES (ninety minutes)

Inductions 1 Including ideodynamics, bridging, deepening, NLP and Munro-Elman fast induction techniques.
Case Tapes Illustrate the use of precision therapy in dealing effectively with a wide range of problems in a single session.

CHILD'S SELF-ESTEEM/SELF-IMAGE TAPE

Letter from a widely-experienced analytical hypnotherapist and biologist:

Child Case 1: 8 years old; nervous tic and cough for three years. Uncovered and dealt with causal factors and both symptoms abated within a week. However, child was still lacking in confidence, clinging to mother and experiencing school problems. The tape was used in the ten days before the second appointment. Bright, bouncy child attended, much more mature, making friends fast at school and earning praise from his hitherto disenchanted teachers. Parents ecstatic, boy ecstatic. Case closed.

Child Case 2: 5 years old; psoriasis and learning problems. Born addicted to heroin. Attention span was measured in seconds. Most emotions (barring anger) locked in and it was a very gruelling session for me. The tape was used for nine nights, apparently on an automatic rewind machine. Second visit, no psoriasis, incredible healing, able to demonstrate his grasp of the alphabet on paper and very proud of the fact that he had not been 'in trouble' at school all week. Session went like a dream and he clearly got rid of a lot of garbage about his mother, and more so of his absent father. Doubt if I could have achieved anything worthwhile without the aid of the tape.

Adult Woman Case 3: Rape at 3 set the pattern for a life of abuse during childhood and considerable self-abuse thereafter. Disastrous relationship with her boyfriend for three years, for both of them. She was tending to behave like a hermit crab in sessions looking out for a few minutes and then disappearing into her shell. Couldn't cope with reviewing early events and then she really got completely stuck. As I saw no other alternative quickly available, I used the 'Child Self Esteem' tape. Very, very damaged child! . . . she loved it! Do did her subconscious! Therapy is really rocketing along now. She has found a job, the relationship with the boyfriend is transformed and she has let go of all her anger towards her mother . . . they are starting to find each other again. Most noticeable feature is that this young woman now manages to laugh and be playful. Her boyfriend is delighted with the change in her. Incredible tape! More anon.

PILGRIM TAPES
P.O. Box 107
Shrewsbury SY1 1ZZ
Tel: (0743) 821270

SUBLIMINAL HEALING MESSAGES

Subliminal recording is not an exact science, which is probably one of the reasons why it is an effective healing medium – feelings enter into it. This can also explain why I cannot explain, even to myself, precisely why some tapes are so effective, particularly when I read that some recognised authority catergorically states that the process I find successful cannot possibly work. A case in point is whether subliminal recordings should be made at 'normal' speaking speed or at accelerated speed, varying from double to thousands of times the normal speaking speed. At accelerated speed, the scripts for twenty or more subjects can be provided, in my case, on a forty-five minute tape labelled 'Multi-Subliminal', with the usual suggestion to subcon to pick out and accept only the plums.

My first tentative approach to the subject was made in 1980 and each step was scientifically planned and executed, starting with recording the bird sounds between 4.15 am and 5 am one spring morning. Unfortunately I found that the recorder had set itself incorrectly with the result that when played back, the tape ran at a quarter speed and the sounds were distorted. The blackbird sounded like Satchmo with a sore throat. It occurred to me that, if I slowed the tape-speed down even more, it might reveal that the birds were actually speaking in Shrewsbury English. After all, they live here. The chirping of the sparrows eventually sounded like dogs barking but the only words I could identify were 'uhuru' and 'asanta sana' in Swahili and a phrase in Gaelic meaning 'mind my harp'. A perceptive colleague said that the thrush seemed to be talking Erse backwards, rather like an improved form of NLP. Anyway, the result was that I was motivated to record my own voice and play it back at varying speeds, passing through the chipmunk stage to a series of sparrow-like chirpings.

One authority has ridiculed the thought that these sounds could be meaningful to the conscious mind and, of course, this is probably correct. This is the level of mind that subliminal messages are designed to bypass anyway and, by masking the low-volume messages with music, they succeed in doing so, at whatever speed.

The human body is variously reported to be made up of fifty trillion to one quadrillian intelligent cells, each one of them capable of five hundred distinct actions and all linked together by a communication system involving fourteen billion channels, at the last count. Big sums apart, it's quite a trick!

Imagine, for a moment, that you could hear the following words as a sound: 'diddely-dah-dit, diddely-dah-dit, did-dah, did-dah, did-dah'. Any Boy Scout and most radio operators will instantly identify this sequence as signalling the start of a message in Morse code, no matter how fast the sequence is transmitted. The 'dits' and 'dahs' that follow, in groups of one to three, are identifiable as letters of the alphabet. The human voice, accelerated, sounds like Morse code. The 'dits' and 'dahs' are sentences, not letters of the alphabet. If the subconscious control mind is, in fact, everything in the universe that the conscious mind is not, it is conceivable that our messages from this vibrational level of reality can be conveyed as coded vibrations, at least at the speed of thought.

Some years after my experiences with the birdbrains and a series of elaborate tests using biomonitoring, a request was received from a London hospital for a subliminal tape to ensure a comfortable delivery for a lady who had problems that could not be dealt with satisfactorily using normal hospital procedure. I was given twenty-four hours to produce the tape. I was aware that my knowledge was inadequate and that the tape messages would be received by all those involved, including the child.

Suffice to say that I was helped to the extent that I mailed the tape within twelve hours knowing that it would be fully effective. It is a double-sided subliminal called 'Gentle Childbirth' and the message is recorded at fifteen decibels below normal audio frequency, at sixty-four times normal speed, masked by music.

An ecstatic doctor telephoned me at 7.30 am two days later to report a trouble-free delivery. 'Everyone is still on Cloud Nine . . . the mother took complete charge . . . six hours passed like one . . . it was a celebration.' He explained that, at one time, a nurse had asked the mother to bear down more strongly. The mother quietly explained that 'my child knows how to be born and when to be born . . . my child is coming into this world gently and easily . . . moving gently within me to be born.' I was quite shaken to hear my own words repeated to me practically verbatim. I had not discussed the script with anyone.

The script is as follows:

DOUBLE-SIDED SUBLIMINAL TAPE – 'GENTLE BIRTH' – for use a few days prior to delivery date

INTRO

Calling on LIFEFORCE to coordinate all levels of mind and being in perfect harmony and balance in a perfect birthing experience when the time is right for the childbearer and for the child, when the time is right for the infant child to be born.

In the first person I speak from the centre of my being for the childbearer in the name of Universal love, in which All is ONE.

All functions of my bodymind system move more and more into harmony and balance with LIFEFORCE, with the one Universal life flow. I relax, I release, I am calm, centred, fully in control. The birth canal is wide and flexible, the pelvic muscles are loose and relaxed in a perfect state of let go . . . the channel to life for a wonderful, happy infant child to be born is FREE – FREE AND CLEAR . . . gently easing my infant child into life . . . the birthing process is EASY, NATURAL and every ten seconds of time passes like one second during the birthing experience. I release, I relax, relaxing every function of the body that eases the way for my infant child. All my thoughts and energies are directed to life-sustaining purpose . . . I am relaxed, calm, centered . . . I am fully in control. I mentally count . . . 1 . . . 2 . . . 3. Relax, relax and I deeply inhale . . . I deeply relax . . . drifting, dreaming, drifting, dreaming . . . feeling so good, so secure, comfortable, comforted, relaxed . . . yet so fully in control . . . at ease with the world, at ease with myself – at ease with everyone. For I am all the love and joy and bliss in LIFE in the fullness of expression . . . peace and peace and peace to everyone . . . LOVE AND LIFE AND LIGHT TO ALL.

My infant child moves with ease through time and space . . . divinely protected – guided by the light and the life and the love within me.

When the time is right . . .

Come gently my child . . . come gently into this wonderful world of consciousness . . . this constant miracle of everyday BEING . . .

Move with ease from within me to be BORN . . . my child . . . to be LOVED . . . to be cherished . . .

Move EASILY from within me, my infant child . . .

> to BE BORN
>
> to BE BORN
>
> to be BORN
>
> to BE BORN TO LOVE

TO LIVE, TO LOVE, TO LAUGH, TO LEARN

to BE BORN . . . to BE BORN . . . WHEN THE TIME IS RIGHT and WELCOME, INFANT CHILD OF THE UNIVERSE . . . a world of LOVE and LIFE and LIGHT awaits you . . .

When the time is right . . .

> Come GENTLY, MY CHILD
>
> COME GENTLY INTO LIFE
>
> TO MY LOVE . . . MY LOVE . . .

The 'Gentle Birth' script is provided with the 'Happy Childbirth' tape and with a note that this is the main part of the subliminal message. This is done with the thought that the expectant mother will assume that relief from pain is also specifically covered. It is not. I was concerned about the omission for a moment when the script evolved and translated itself spontaneously onto tape. Happily, I was motivated to go with the feeling and not with my thoughts.

The 'Rapid Relaxation' tape is recommended as part of the set. On one occasion a client was momentarily upset when a midwife said: 'Surely you are feeling some pain.' A mild form of the Esdaile state is provided on the RR tape to ensure that self-limiting negative conditioning is ineffective and that creative awareness and mental, emotional and physical equilibrium is maintained.

The reports and letters on the results of the tapes make joyful reading and repeatedly mention another aspect. The child is unusually independent. Julia, for example, a mother of three, wrote: 'Young Henry is a very independent little soul. Being fed . . . baby chair . . . baby cot . . . baby anything . . . they are not for him.' Another lad, born naturally, at home, showed similar self-assurance, to the extent that on the day that he first walked, he wandered over to a neighbour's house and knocked on the door. The neighbour brought him back home. 'I'm sorry,' she told his mother. 'I couldn't understand what he was saying. I think he was asking me if I could come out to play.'

The baby photographs I receive touch a part of my nature that I would otherwise never have known existed. I feel that it has to be a two-way channel. Those youngsters must chortle a lot.

FERTILITY TAPE

The Pilgrim fertility tape has scored a high percentage of successes where other forms of treatment, including protracted hypnoanalysis, have been unsuccessful.

One successful tape case provided an interesting sidelight on the subject. The lady client became pregnant less than three months after she and her husband started listening to the tape, a hypno-subliminal. On checking my files, I found that both of them had completed a Lüscher test for me. The lady's selections showed no evidence of a problem. The husband's selection reflected moderate stress (he is a police officer) and (=01) . . . a seemingly harmless couplet which personal experience has repeatedly revealed indicates the possible existence of a serious physiological/emotional problem. The advantage, with taped therapy . . . and particularly with this type of problem ... is that the message reaches both partners.

A test recheck showed that the husband's problem had cleared. Every indication is that at least eighty percent of our health problems can resolve themselves automatically if we learn to relax creatively for five minutes a day.

There also seems to be a penalty for offences against Nature and offences against a mother-to-be rank high on the list. This impression was reinforced, for me, in one case of infertility when the lady client responded evasively to the stock question ... 'do you want your husband to be the father of your child?' The first response was: 'If we don't have one now, we never will ... I'm forty.' The second: 'He has always wanted a son.' Three more evasions followed. Halfway through the fourth, the lady sobbed bitterly: 'He hits me when he gets drunk.' Later, regressing her to the night before her first miscarriage revealed that her husband came home drunk and they had a row, in which she was hit. The scenario for her second miscarriage two years later was identical. Seemingly Nature had decided that twice was enough. Her husband was not amenable to therapy, taped or otherwise.

FERTILITY PROBLEMS

The following is the text of the professional newsletter issued on the subject in 1990:

Natural Fertility

A study of the authoritative literature on the subject of infertility reveals that five of the six factors that contribute to health problems are overlooked, the mental, emotional, sensory, environmental and chemical influences. Concentration is focused on the 'identifiable causes' which are reported to include hormonal imbalance, defective ovaries, internal malfunctions, 'genetic problems' and low sperm count ... all of which are clearly symptoms rather than causes. In concentrating on eliminating symptoms, it is hardly surprising to learn that the doctrinaire approach to infertility can claim a success rate of less than twenty per cent. This result is possibly less than the rate of success to be expected in allowing the natural recuperative processes to function without the stress and indignity of exposure to chemical and mechanical intervention.

Nevertheless, there is invariably a three or more months' waiting list for 'high-tech' IVF treatment, costing from £9,000 to £12,000. This can involve X-rays, hysteroscopy (telescopic inspection of the uterus), laparoscopy (inspection through a small hole made in the stomach) and ultrasonic scanning. The secondary effect of these intrusions on the bodymind system is not the subject of study.

Resolving infertility problems with the hypno-analytical process is often more personally and professionally rewarding than dealing with the wide range of other living problems that therapists encounter. Any one or several of the emotional insight-stimulation techniques can be effectively used, from fast-track pinpointing and ideodynamic processes to the gentler scenic-route approaches involving free association and age-regression.

The first four infertility cases encountered in analysis by my associate and me were dealt with successfully as a matter of course. The fact that reproductive problems were a matter of concern was only revealed in working with the clients on their other declared problems.

The professional advantage, apart from the relative ease with which the undesirable state yields to the release of inhibitory emotions, is that evidence of the success of the therapy is usually available within eight to ten weeks. The delighted parents-to-be become strong advocates of analytical hypnotherapy for life.

There is also a bonus for the new generation. In experiencing how parental neuroses and other childhood influences can sow the seeds for our problems in later life, the parents-to-be are better placed to avoid passing on to their children our common genetic inheritance . . . our inheritance of self-limiting negative conditioning.

UNDERSTANDING PARENTS

Originally designed to eliminate the false feelings of guilt entertained by children of divorced parents, this tape has proved useful in this and many other cases. One involved a request for the 'Cancel Cancer' tape for a four-month-old infant with spinal cancer. Forgetting that we are all equally mature at the subcon level and concerned about the strength of the 'Cancel Cancer' tape, I sent the 'Understanding Parents' tape and asked the father to advise me on how his son responded. Other parents had reported that their children had adopted the foetal position on hearing side 'B'. My intention was to offer the heavier tape if the infant responded in a similar way.

Eight weeks later the father telephoned to report that his son had moved for the first time in his life on hearing the tape. 'Umpteen playings' and four weeks later, a scan revealed that the tumour had gone. A second scan had confirmed this and the infant showed every evidence of exuberant good health. I checked the script several times before I saw how the affirmations could stimulate this type of response. It does nothing for my ego to realise that my best scripts owe nothing to my intelligence.

CANCEL CANCER SET

The full set has been used successfully by survivors from the age of ten. It includes CCI, CCII and CC double-sided subliminal. The latter is available either as a musical subliminal or as a whisper.

CCII was intended to be the eighth update of CCI, to include a theme that evolved in dealing successfully, in therapy, with a brain-tumour case. A double-sided ninety-minute hypnosis tape usually requires forty to forty-six A4 pages of narrative. The update started as intended but around page six the script took over and started writing itself and an entirely new theme evolved . . . a very powerful theme. So much so, that several clients, including two who live within a few hundred miles of Shrewsbury, have found it unnecessary to visit for therapy. The tapes alone have dealt with their cancer problems, fast and effectively.

MEDICAL COMA RELEASE TAPE

In much the same way that an individual sealed against conscious hypnosis, either by accident or by design, will respond to a subliminal message, a hospital patient who had been in a medical coma for five weeks responded within hours to a subliminal tape request to communicate, using ideodynamic signals. A born traditionalist, I originally sought to have the index finger, right hand, rise to signify 'Yes' and the little finger, to indicate 'No'. Focusing on this, I was nearly knocked off my chair by her left foot. It shot out from under the bedclothes. Her left hand movements signified 'No'. In response to my first question: 'Do you want to return to everyday living reality?' . . . the response was a clear 'Yes' . . . and 'No'. I dislike 'Twenty Questions' as a game and it took me nearly two hours to establish the cause of the problem and the action required to release the lady from the coma. This included explaining to her (too doting) husband that she had been planning to leave him and his discovery that one of their bank accounts had been relieved of £20,000 had seemingly triggered the coma as a means of escape. He had dutifully spent at least four hours a day by her bedside when she went into the coma. Communication was established between husband and wife using ideodynamic signalling and she was encouraged to come out of the coma.

It was clearly established by the client's responses that the diamorphine and the phenytoin which were being administered daily had contributed towards the perforation of the walls of the urethra and the bowel, providing an unusual channel for the release of diarrhoea. The diamorphine was being administered in the mistaken belief that the whimpering sounds emitted by the patient were indications of pain. They were, in fact, attempts to communicate.

Questioning confirmed that the immobility of the limbs on the right side was the result of a mild stroke that had preceded the coma. The medical staff were extremely helpful, even to the extent of providing a list of the possible side effects of the drugs being used but they were disinclined to accept my offer of the coma access tape to communicate with other patients. The offer, coupled with instructions in communicating more easily with medical coma victims, is still open.

Subsequent experience has confirmed the value of the coma release tape but pacing techniques alone have sometimes proved effective. Whatever verbal sounds the coma victim is producing, from whimpers to screams, seem to be an attempt to communicate their thoughts and feelings. By imitating the sounds and gradually introducing normal speech patterns, the coma victim can be induced to communicate intelligibly. The same applies to communicating with schizoidal clients when the ego-state adopts a slowed-down or distorted speech pattern. A modified version of the medical coma release tape has also proved useful in communicating with schizophrenics and clients diagnosed as suffering from M.E.

STRESS RELIEF TAPE

The stress relief tape, in one form or another, has proved successful in initiating and sometimes necessarily completing the process of restoring highly stressed clients to mental and emotional harmony and balance. They regularly include genuinely suicidal clients, who can readily be identified with the Lüscher colour test.

Social Service staff have provided me with valuable insights in developing the various approaches to taped stress relief. To help them in their work, I invariably introduce them to the Lüscher test. On one occasion, just one day after one of my presentations to a group of twenty Social Service workers, one staff-member telephoned to say that she had tested the people she had visited that morning and was rather unimpressed with the results. A lady client she knew well had selected (+74) twice, indicating strong suicidal tendencies. The lady had been signed-off that very morning by the psychiatrist after three months treatment. On my suggestion, she revisited the lady that afternoon, who admitted making arrangements to end it all that evening . . . and showed how. Before my friend left, the client's daughter, a senior nurse, arrived to see her mother. She greeted the Social Service worker with: 'What do you think you are doing here? Mother was discharged from care this morning. Can't you people leave her alone?'

In this, as in countless other similar situations, the stress relief tape alone has proved sufficient to provide the confused person with better options than self-destruction. Lüscher tests reveal that stress levels decrease from eight or higher to two in less than two months. One session of precision analysis can, of course, accelerate the recovery process for those who seek effective help.

Having experienced the state myself it helps . . . in retrospect . . . to accept that suicide is the sincerest form of self-criticism. I have heard that, on one occasion, a poet was advised that another aspiring poet he knew had committed suicide. 'I never realised,' he said, 'that he was so public-spirited.'

A British counselling magazine featured an article on the subject in March 1993. A case study of a suicidal woman was provided to illustrate 'the kind of work that can be done', explaining that all the elements of despair, isolation, anger and helplessness 'are projected into the counsellor who must then act as a container'. The client, it was reported, is not cured, 'as she still gets depressed and has suicidal thoughts'. The counsellor has 'placed her professional expertise at her disposal by applying important theoretical understandings', with the objective of illustrating that life is worth living. 'The woman was severely suicidal when she first presented herself for therapy four years ago. She has been having twice-weekly sessions ever since.'

KEEP TAKING THE TAPELETS: THINGS PEOPLE SAY

- 'You explained that, as I learn to find greater trust in myself, I will know when to trust others. I have been "listening" to your inaudible whisper subliminals. What greater trust is there than that?'

  (Listening to subliminals masked by music, madam! The whisper subliminals are 'unmasked' . . . the accelerated-speech process can be reversed to provide the original script. As a subliminal, it bypasses the superficial doubting levels of mind).

- 'Can you provide me with a subliminal tape without the sound of waves, please. I hear them sixteen hours a day. Docking sounds would be very acceptable.'

  (Shell tanker captain, South China Seas station, at anchor in Tokyo Bay).

- 'I am an octogenarian. Your tape has helped me with my arthritis. I am eighty percent better.'

- Male client: 'As I suffered from bruxism, I had to have a bra fitted.'

  (A trade term, apparently, for a bite-raising appliance).

- An African medical student, who returned home for a month in 1993, telephoned me from London to explain that his father had been intrigued to find that his English vocabulary had expanded in many ways since using a double-sided subliminal tape that his student son had sent him. He was even more astonished when his son played the hypnotic equivalent. He recognised the phraseology that he had acquired subliminally.

  The student wrote the following letter from London, giving written permission to quote it:

There are a dozen stories to tell you . . . how about this one:
When I arrived home, I learned that my father's best friend for
thirty years had been in a coma for three months. He had fallen
from a crowded bus, sustaining minor lacerations and bruises.
Doctors had diagnosed brain damage and he had already lived
longer than had been predicted. Despite heavy scepticism from
family and friends, his wife undertook to play the self-healing
tape to him. Two days later he sat up in bed and called to his
wife. Celebrations followed all round and his eldest son, a
senior military officer, threw a party for everyone that lasted a
week.

I barely escaped with your self-healing tape, secretly enjoying my new dignatory title of "Mister Wonderman"!

I could write for ever, but first things first. I need one more
intensive training session with you on precision therapy, then
I'm off home. The scope for a first-class therapist in (country) is
immense . . . both for healing and training others. It is work I
can truly enjoy and . . . the good news . . . my father fully
approves.

- A letter from Aberdeen: 'I received a copy of your "Love Awareness" tape from a friend of mind.'

- 'I have spent years trying to find the real me. Your "Lifelines"
tape told me to relax and stop trying, then the real me found me.'

- 'Your diagnostic technique (the Lüscher test) has that essential
personal touch that the medical profession lost when they made
the great mistake of abandoning the probing finger down the
throat and the stiff finger up the rectum.
I can thoroughly accept its validity though it is away outside my
personal comfort zone and still travelling.'

- 'Could you speak slower on your whisper subliminals so that I
can hear what you are telling me when I'm in bed?'

- Son to father: 'Why didn't you tell me there is a whisper subliminal that you turn down so that you hear nothing? I wouldn't feel
so bad when I wake up in the morning and find I forgot to switch
on the "Study – Pass Exams" hypnosis tape last night.'

- 'Our dog loves your voice. He goes to sleep the moment we start
playing your tapes.'

- 'Your tinnitus tape has cured my arthritis . . . have you any other
suggestions?' (Label change imminent).

- Analyst reports: 'Using your "Creative Dreampower" tape recently. Dreamt I was travelling, passed through Customs all right, Immigration took my passport, tore the pages out, handed it back, let me through. Worked on the dream for half-an-hour, failed to extract any meaning. First lady-client of the day arrived. "Here's last night's dream," she said. "You asked me to write it down. Hardly worth it. I was travelling, passed through Customs OK, Immigration took my passport, then let me through." "Did they tear any pages out of it?" "Of course not, it's my passport!" "Sit down, please . . . and just relax" etc. The analyst read the note as soon as his client left. "Dreamt I was travelling, passed through Customs all right, Immigration took my passport, tore the pages out, handed it back, let me through." Analyst's complaint cancelled. It wasn't his dream.

- 'Child Self Esteem' stories? There are hundreds.

  One eighty-four-year-old healer in London was motivated by the tape to return to an eight-hour working day.

  An analyst insists that all his clients hear it at home once, at least. 'It's the only message that I know everyone can relate to. I can.'

  Caroline wrote: 'I returned from a heavy business trip with a severe middle ear infection . . . (there's a lot I didn't want to hear!) The three children sat down with me in a circle. They insisted: "We will sit together as One." They then blasted me with mental sunlight, leaving me with no alternative. I recovered overnight.' Complaint from Jennifer: 'I fall asleep before I hear the story of the little lion.' 'Then, set the tape to start just before that part begins!' 'Then I won't hear you calling me "Wonderchild of the Universe!"' (Five-minute tape upcoming).

- Judith is one of those unsung heroines who daily introduces thirty five-year-old children to schoolwork. The 'Child Esteem' tapes are a daily favourite. On one occasion, a local police sergeant gave them a video presentation of the contribution the police make to the welfare of the community, concluding with a question: 'If you are ever in any kind of trouble and your Mummy and Daddy aren't there to help you . . . who is the one person you can call on for help?' He was stunned by a loud chorus of 'Duncan'.

- The following is an extract from a letter from Nicola about her five-year-old daughter Anne, who had been causing problems both at home and at school. The teacher apparently telephoned to enquire what had been done to make such a dramatic change in the child's behaviour. She was now attentive in class and could count backwards as fast as forwards, always insisting on finishing with a triumphant 'zero . . . zero . . . ZERO'.

● A photograph of a glamorous Polish mother with her baby son in her arms, graces my study windowsill, one of a dozen or so inspiring reminders of joyful events in which my tapes participated. The lady's twelve-year-old son telephoned me on his own initiative to tell me that he had a new baby brother, born the previous night, and everything had gone fine. He was leaving shortly to visit the hospital with his father and wondered which tape he should take with him for his new brother. Not knowing which tapes he had, I asked: 'What would you suggest?' Tad said: 'Excel at Sport.'

The fact is that, out of the seventy public-list tapes, 'Excel at Sport' provides perhaps the best recipe for enjoying a happy, healthy, productive lifestyle.

● One of the morbid fears enjoyed by state-of-the-ark neo-Freudian analysts is that hypnosis tapes featuring regression techniques may create transference and varying degrees of attachment (or *cassettitis*). To a degree, the fear is justified. In my own experience, I still have a high regard for mind-master Barrie Konicov, whose tapes helped me to shed thirty years of scoliosis and four years of spinal cancer. Perhaps the enlightening message I received from a five-year-old girl in a Sheffield school can dispel the self-limiting negative conditioning.

She was one of thirty children who sent me a thank-you card for the 'Child Esteem' tape they had all heard in class. I thanked them, in turn, for their cards by sending them one large one in which I had featured all their names as anagrams: LEKY for Kyle, AMOTHS for Thomas, etc, saying that I had dropped the alphabet.

An ongoing series: another bunch of hand-painted cards arrived from the children, the enlightening message from CABECER read:

> 'I have found myself Duncan.
> I can skip Duncan.
> Rebecca'

Quotations

Potential forms of Consciousness

Our normal waking consciousness, rational consciousness as we call it, is but one special type of consciousness, whilst all about it, parted from it by the filmiest of screens, there lie potential forms of consciousness entirely different . . . No account of the universe in its totality can be final which leaves these other forms of consciousness quite disregarded . . . they forbid a premature closing of our accounts with reality.

William James

Any Land You Choose

Bid your soul travel to any land you choose and sooner than you bid it go, it will be there. Bid it fly up to heaven, and it will not lack for wings. Nothing can bar its way, neither the fiery heat of the sun, nor the swirl of the planet-spheres. Cleaving its way through all, it will fly up till it reaches the outermost of all corporeal things. And should you wish to break forth from the universe itself and gaze on the things outside the cosmos, even that is permitted to you. See what power, what quickness is yours.

Hermes Trismegistus

A Long Time

It takes one a long time to become young.

Pablo Picasso

Waiting for Some Power

Men have never fully used
the powers they possess
to advance the good in life,
because they have waited upon
some power external to themselves
and to nature
to do the work
they are responsible for doing.

John Dewey

A Single Reality

As a result of my experiences, I believe that I exist not only in the

196

familiar world of space and time, but also in a realm having a timeless, eternal quality. Behind the apparent multiplicity of things in the world of science and common sense, there is a single reality in which all things are united. (For example, it seems quite possible for people to communicate telepathically, without any use of sight or hearing, since deep down our minds are all connected anyway.)

W. Harman

What We Suppressed

Along with rediscovering our feelings and wants, is to recover our relation with the subconscious aspects of ourselves ... As modern man has given up sovereignty over his body, so also he has surrendered the unconscious side of his personality, and it has become almost alien to him ... we need to find and welcome back, so far as we can, what we suppressed.

Rollo May

The Pyramid of Memory

Our memories, at any given moment, form a solid whole, a pyramid, so to speak, whose point is inserted precisely into our present action. But behind the memories which are concerned in our present occupation and are revealed by means of it, there are others, thousands of others, stored below the scene illuminated by consciousness. Yes, I believe indeed that all our past life is there, preserved even to the most infinitesimal details, and that we forget nothing, and that all that we have felt, perceived, thought, willed, from the first awakening of our consciousness, survives indestructibly.

Henri Bergson

Spring

I know where the windflowers blow! I know. I have been where the little rabbits run, I and warm yellow sun!

Diane Jurkovic, Grade 2

P.S. 148, Queens

Through the Problem

Release in extremity
lies through
and not away from
the problem

Alan Watts

Time's Relativity

When you sit with a nice girl for two hours you think it's only a minute. But when you sit on a hot stove for a minute you think it's two hours. That's relativity.

Albert Einstein

The Focus of Motivation

Hypnotism has a startling capacity to step up motivation in the human being, to step up his motor, his driving power. In many cases, the human being is a failure because like Don Quixote he jumps on his horse and rides off madly in all directions at the same time. He does not channel his energy. With hypnotism, we can set up what we term a monomotivational field, wherein the energies of the individual are firmly pointed in one certain direction, with the exclusion of side issues and distractions.

G.H. Estabrooks

Hidden in My Interior

I am fully aware of the fact that the mental state I am in has nothing to do with my usual mental state. I am no more the same man; I do not see or feel in the same way as before. I feel I have a double personality or, rather, as if one other person hidden in my deeper interior had suddenly emerged and replaced my normal personality. But yet, it does not seem to me that my usual thinking is entirely destroyed; this is certainly not the case. But beneath the surface of my conscious intelligence which directs my usual life, I feel there lives and works a subconscious intelligence, which is faster and more comprehensive than this one . . .

de Fleuriere

Through Consciousness

Through becoming conscious we have been driven out of paradise, through consciousness we can come back to paradise.

Heinrich Jacoby

Allowing Us to Hear

We turn on a radio and hear
an orchestra playing
Vienna Bonbons,
and of course the music was there
in the room all the time,
and the music would be there
even if the radio were not;
the radio simply allows us
to hear the music.

William Braden

A Point of Passage

The organism is never located in a single instant. In its life the three modes of time – the past, the present and the future – form a whole which cannot be split up into individual elements . . . We cannot describe the momentary state of an organsim without taking its history into consideration and without referring it to a future state for which this state is merely a point of passage.

Ernst Cassirer

A New Frontier

I saw that if I could go 50 years ahead, everybody would leave me alone. And that's exactly the way it happened. I was allowed to do anything I wanted and people said, 'Well, you're very amusing, but obviously I can't take you seriously.' But because I'd deliberately got to living and thinking 50 years ahead on a comprehensive basis, I inadvertently got myself into a strange position. I began to live on that frontier, and it was like any wave phenomenon: I was living where it was cresting and things happened to me long before they happened to the rest of society.

R. Buckminster Fuller

Training the Human Instrument

Concentration has neither ethical nor spiritual value, and calls for no special time or place or posture for practicing. The exercises correspond to those which a ballet dancer must use before the simplest dance can be performed, or to the earnest young pianist's scales, or the fencer's early lessons in precision of aim. Only when the executive instrument, be it the limb, the hands, or the machinery of thought, has been brought under control of the will, can the art itself be effectively developed.

Christmas Humphreys

Born Free

Compulsion is being trapped in a known psychic reality, a dead-end space. Freedom is in the unknown. If you believe there is an unknown everywhere, in your own body, in your relationships with other people, in political institutions, in the universe, then you have maximum freedom. If you can examine old beliefs and realize they are limits to be overcome and can also realize you don't have to have a belief about something you don't yet know anything about, you are free.

John C. Lilly

The Self in Past and Future

Psyche is transition, hence necessarily to be defined under two aspects. On the one hand, the psyche gives a picture of the remnants and traces of the entire past, and, on the other, but expressed in the same picture, the outlines of the future, inasmuch as the psyche creates its own future.

C.G. Jung

Cosmic Consciousness

The prime characteristic of cosmic consciousness is, as its name implies, a consciousness of the cosmos, that is, of the life and order of the universe . . . Along with this there occurs an intellectual enlightenment or illumination which alone would place the individual on a new plane of existence – would make him almost a member of a new species. To this is added a state of moral exaltation, an indescribable feeling of elevation, elation, and joyousness, and a quickening of the moral sense, which is fully striking and more important both to the individual and to the race than is the enhanced intellectual power. With these come what may be called a sense of immortality, a consciousness of eternal life, not conviction that he shall have this, but the consciousness that he has it already.

R.M. Bucke

Your Genuine, Deepest Self

Show me your original face which you had before your father and mother conceived you! Show me – in other words – your genuine, deepest self, not the self which depends on family and conditioning, on learning or experience, or any kind of artifice.

Alan Watts

The Secrets of Great Men

This art of resting the mind and the power of dismissing from it all care and worry is probably one of the secrets of energy in our great men.

Captain J.A. Hadfield

Together in Yourself

Find your home in the haunts of every living creature. Make yourself higher than all heights and lower than all depths. Bring together in yourself all opposites of quality: heat and cold, dryness and fluidity. Think that you are everywhere at once, on land, at sea, in heaven. Think that you are not yet begotten, that you are in the womb, that you are young, that you are old, that you have died, that you are in the world beyond the grave. Grasp in your thought all this at once, all times and places, all substances and qualities and magnitudes together. Then you can apprehend God.

Hermes Trismegistus

True Awakening

The aim of the game is true awakening, full development of the powers latent in man. The game can be played only by people whose observations of themselves and others have led them to a certain conclusion, namely, that man's ordinary state of consciousness, his so-called waking state, is not the highest level of consciousness of which he is capable. In fact, this state is so far from real awakening that it could appropriately be called a form of somnambulism, a condition of 'waking sleep.'

Robert S. DeRopp

Pilgrims Together

Life is so full of meaning and purpose, so full of beauty – beneath its covering – that you will find that earth but cloaks your heaven. Courage, then, to claim it – that is all. But courage you have, and the knowledge that we are pilgrims together, wending through unknown country, home.

Fra Giovanni

PAST LIVES – FACT OR FICTION?

'All I can see are stone walls,' she sobbed, 'stone walls and four stone pillars . . . oval shaped pillars, no windows . . . it's a cell . . . a dungeon.' a moment later she spoke the name of the town and the cathedral. The lady client had regressed to a 'previous experience' . . . a 'PLE'. Condemned for witchcraft by the villagers, she was destined to experience a fiery send-off.

This was a fairly widely publicised case, one of hundreds of PLE cases described by a famous hypnotherapist in the 1950s. The then bishop of the particular cathedral confirmed that there were many cells in the cathedral but none with oval shaped pillars. Some months later, he wrote to report that during renovations a wall in the basement had been demolished revealing additional cells. In one there were four oval pillars.

Anedoctal evidence, of course, like all the best and worst religious themes and to an analytical hypnotherapist limited to neo-Freudian concepts, the experience is automatically categorised as cryptomnesia . . . something possibly overheard or seen on the Late Night Show as a child . . . a trick of the mind, a fluke.

The first PLE that surfaced for me in therapy involved a teenager who, despite her slight build, could react violently with jealousy. In one jealousy-provoking incident she described, involving an elder sister, I was prompted to ask, 'Where is your mother?' 'She died six years ago.' Her mother was in fact browsing through magazines in the adjoining waiting-room.

Five other PLE incidents followed one after the other, all of them prime-time soap-opera material. In one experience she was farmer's wife, middle-aged, speaking with a truly rural accent. She said she had been married for 16 years. 'Have you any children'? I asked, just to enter into the game. 'How can oi 'ave chillun and get all my chores done too then?' She started to sob. It seemed that her husband had run away with a woman who could do both . . . and the seeds of jealousy were sown.

An associate recently experienced a more dramatic PLE response with a client suffering from asthma. Asthma is usually easy to relieve permanently, using analysis techniques to bring the initial sensitising event and any subsequent compounding experiences to consciousness. The sensitivity is usually seeded in the gestation period and is compounded at or shortly after birth, often involving problems with the umbilical cord.

My associate's case was different. The client's head suddenly twisted to one side. He gurgled 'I'm spinning . . . spinning round. Blurred faces.' Then realisation 'I'm being hanged!' The effect of the emotional release was immediately apparent. 'For the first time in my life . . . I can breathe without wheezing.

Richard was a paratrooper until recently, battle-seasoned in one of the elite fighting-groups in which the training was designed to be more stressful than war. Establishing two-way communication with the controls levels of his mind, an indication was given that a pre-conception experience was the sensitising event of his major problems. In a PLE lasting sixty seconds, Richard found himself embroiled in a clan battle with great clashings of swords and raucous battle-cries and surrounded by men seemingly revelling in the slaughter. Richard was not. This was not his thing. He was a gentleman and a dandy . . . a ladies' man. As the noise and the battle intensified around him, he turned his head just in time to see a bright orange sphere growing larger as it sped towards him . . . a red-hot cannon-ball.

'Nasty,' I said. 'No,' he smiled, 'wonderful. I have such a sense of realease and freedom. I don't have to play soldier anymore. I can be as brave as the next man without pretending to revel in it. I don't have to act like my Dad – he has always been a hard man, proud that he was the youngest sergeant in the Tank Corps in 1941, a regular soldier. 'Regular,' he laughed, with a sob in his voice, 'Lord love him . . . I can see it all now, he was probably as scared stiff as me!'

Sometimes there is a hint that a PLE is perhaps the only way for the controls levels of the mind to bypass the barriers of thought, to enable us to regain perspective, to permit us to stand far enough back from our involvement to see the whole story and to allow our true feelings to vent . . . to allow our feelings to reach beyond the false limits of memory and linear-controlled thought.

A senior member of one of the major cancer research foundations recently visited me from the USA to discuss healing concepts and therapy results. He attributed his own success in eliminating his pancreatic cancer to a macrobiotic diet he had adopted since 1980. A brief analysis confirmed that he was fairly healthy and, more for the experience than for any specific benefit, he asked to be regressed to an earlier life. This proved to be unusually easy and he was impressed by the intensity of the experience. 'I was standing alone on the shore, watching a prison ship leaving for Australia. It was a large, ugly, three-masted boat. I felt this deep sense of personal loss, I don't know why. Wait a minute,' he gasped, 'I see it all now. When I "went holistic" twenty years ago, I lost the doctorate I had held for forty years and I lost all my professional friends . . . they didn't want to know me. I couldn't reach them . . . their minds were imprisoned. I shrugged it all off as part of the price I had to pay for freedom of action. What I didn't know until now was that I didn't shrug it off from "down under". I have been hurting deep-down all the time.' (He is an active man with an agile, enquiring mind – young at 85).

When you learn how to apply your own powers of conscious self-hypnosis, you awaken to the realisation that our conscious state of mind is, in fact, one of unconscious self-hypnosis. As a natural human state, self-hypnosis fails to meet the scientific criteria that it must be capable of being proved in theory. As in healing and love, and all things natural, an element of the unknown and the unintentional enters into it.

Zen understanding has, long ago, revealed that a child's character is formed hundreds of years before the parents are born. Effective hypnoanalysis can confirm that our behaviour is largely governed by our 'genetic encoding', by the imprint of thoughts on the embryo or on egg cells in the womb. Consequently, a spontaneous remission is never an accident. It is the result of an abrupt shift in personal awareness. At a creative level of relaxation, the shift in awareness can be caused.

A doctrinaire or intellectually-swamped mind can have difficulty in befriending the feeling of living comfortably without neat answers. True or false, it turns out, have no relevance in healing. What counts is the psychic effect.

Points on Heavier Problems

The following letter was received in 1991 from a tape client in Germany, headed: 'Cancer, a conflict of the psyche, made visible by brain scan images':

This letter concerns every living soul and should at least be read and stored away in one's memory bank, because this letter is about the medicine of tomorrow. It will revolutionise medicine in 5, 10 or 30 years, depending on how long the present orthodox cancer research is financed by a willing public. We are reaching the year 2000 and your prospects of dying from cancer are on the increase, instead of a reversed trend. The real tragedy for today's cancer victims is that many of them would have a chance to survive and recover. Read now about the extraordinary medical discoveries by Dr G.R. Hamer.

A widely-respected and successful German doctor shocked the medical establishment in 1982 with his documented evidence that cancer is always triggered by a psychological conflict which causes a bioletic short in very specific regions of the brain. Dr Hamer presented 200 case histories, each accompanied by brain-scans or CTs (computer tonographs). This is a relatively new type of X-ray process, which produces a much higher degree of detail than the conventional X-ray images. The brain CTs of these 200 case histories show shadowing circles which Dr Hamer refers to as 'Hamer Focal'.

The fascinating part of this discovery is the photographic proof of psychosomatic interactions. The healer knows very well that most illnesses, including cancer, have their origin in the 'soul' of the person; however, healers had no means of making effects of the healing messages immediately visible.

Orthodox medicine of course prefers to ignore the 'invisible soul factor' for therapy. Instead, chemotherapy, radiation and radical surgery are the major treatment cornerstones for cancer.

Dr Hamer tried desperately to gain recognition for his 'New Medicine'. Up until 1986 he already had accumulated documentary evidence of thousands of case histories. By then, the German Medical Society revoked Dr Hamer's licence to practise medicine. His method was too much for orthodox medicine – it would have meant too many upheavals. Instead of pumping a patient full of drugs or performing surgery, the doctor would have to spend 2–3 hours talking to a patient and almost like a detective find out the shock event which led to the brain-short and triggered the cancer.

According to Hamer, cancer is a very common event in the human body. It may be caused instantly by a shock event and it may be healing soon after through the body's immune system. The course of cancer is always:

(1) Psychic imprint;
(2) Brain response;
(3) Physical manifestation.

The brain-scan image provides a wealth of diagnostic information:

- If the patient has had cancers in the past, which were healed and which organs were affected.

- If the patient suffers from cancer now and which organs are affected.

- The scan also yields information on the stage of the cancer process:
    (1) active cancer growth;
    (b) healing phase.

- According to Dr Hamer instant healing sets in when the psychological conflict is recognised and the patient comes to terms with it.

- The conflict: most conflicts come down to a very basic content; loss of a loved one, infringement on one's terrain, etc.

The conflicting/shocking influence hits one of the three brain centres, depending on the type of information (see 'Evolution of the Brain', below).

THE EVOLUTION OF THE BRAIN

The human brain evolved from animal life over hundreds of millions of years. In the course of evolution, three basic brain control centres evolved:

Brain centre	Related cell structure	Related symbiotic life forms
1. Ancient brain	Entoderm	Virus
2. Minor brain	Mesoderm	Bacteria
3. Major brain	Ectoderm	Fungus

THE HAMER SYNDROME

When psychological conflict hits the brain, this phenomenal biological computer directs the message to any one of the brain centres which is geared-up to deal with the situation. If the shock hits the person unexpectedly, when the person is exhausted or particularly vulnerable, the brain cannot deal with the situation and the brain element suffers an electrical short, which immediately becomes visible on the brain-scan as 'Hamer Focal'. At the same time, related organ-cells in the body become cancerous. The relationship between brain cells and organ-cells stems from the early primitive life forms when there were no distinctions between brain and body cells.

AUTONOMOUS HEALING OF CANCERS

A resilient person fights the cancer autonomously and without being aware. The related symbiotic life forms (virus, bacteria, fungi), come into action and attack the cancerous growth. Orthodox medicine treats these life forms as enemies although they have been part of our bodies for hundreds of millions of years.

Antibodies, inoculations, etc., are effectively killing off the natural symbiotic friends of the human race. Cancer is not healed by medical intervention, it is fostered by it.

HEALING OF THE UNDERLYING CAUSE, THE PSYCHE

Dr Hamer's patients experienced instant healing when the underlying conflict was identified and the patient came to terms with it.

HEALING WITH MENTAL POWERS, HYPNOTHERAPY, YOGA ETC.

Nothing needs to be added to these concepts as they are widely publicised. The achievement of Dr Hamer is that he can produce visible proof of the cause of the cancer in the body, telegraphed by the brain. Dr Hamer's book is to be published in the English language in the later part of 1991 by his own publishing company:

AMICI DI Dirk
Sulzburgstrasse 29
5000 Köln 41
Germany

AUTHOR'S NOTE

My information, at present, is that Dr Hamer was unable to arrange to have the book printed.

*   *   *

Following a visit in March 1993 by the head of an international cancer research team on his return to Europe from discussions with Drs Bernie Siegel and Carl Simonton in the USA, I learned that the findings of Dr Ryke Geerd Hamer of Cologne have been authenticated by other medical authorities in Germany and the diagnostic techniques have been successfully adopted by ASAC (Association Stop to Cancer) in Chamberg, France.

Providing visual evidence of the influence of emotions may serve to interest a wider audience in the hypnoanalytical process but, like using biomonitoring equipment while working with a client in analysis, it introduces an unnecessary distraction. The evidence that the client is creatively relaxed and that the dramatic shift in personal awareness that stimulates healing has been achieved is always abundantly clear to both parties.

There is a second point which may or may not be significant. In many types of problem including cancer and cystic fibrosis, repeated indications are that the bodymind controls can cope fairly adequately with the effects of medicinal chemicals but they have difficulty in dealing with the damage caused by any form of scanning or radiation treatment.

A more useful discovery in 1993 was that a Dr Winkler in Louisiana, USA, is using fairly rapid hypnoanalytical techniques similar to those described in this book, and he can also substantiate a success rate with cancer cases in excess of ninety percent. He was able to report 84 successes out of 89 cases in 1992. Asked why he found it difficult to get the message of his success across to the medical fraternity, he referred to the dramatic work of a Dr Dabnly in Louisiana, who uses rapid hypnotic induction and suggestion techniques to stimulate and accelerate healing in serious industrial burns cases. Unlike a cancer specialist, Dr Dabnly can illustrate the remarkable results of his work with dramatic videotaped evidence. As consultant-on-call to metal foundries and chemical plants, his experience includes dealing with victims of explosions and molten-metal spills.

The ideal, as Dr Dabnly explains, is to have access to induct the patient immediately or at least within two hours of an accident. This is possible if the treating physician on an emergency case has been trained in using simple induction techniques. Dr Dabnly trains the first-aid teams in the companies which use his services but adequate access to the patient may sometimes be delayed for six hours or more. Even in these cases, the influence of the accelerated healing-effect of the hypnotic suggestions is clearly evidenced. The complications of swelling, blistering, infection and the need for skin grafts are avoided and no evidence of a third-degree burn remains . . . the epidermis forms and the burned skin and tissue heal naturally.

Dr Dabnly's video records illustrate the progress in healing in dozens of cases, including accidents in which a leg was immersed in molten zinc at 370°C and an arm (different man!) was exposed to a 3000°C flame when an acetylene-torch hose was cut. In the molten zinc case, the epidermis reformed seventeen days after the accident, there was no swelling and, four years later, the injured leg was indistinguishable from the other leg, even to the extent that normal hair growth had been re-established.

Dr Dabnly tells that, on one occasion, while following a group of doctors out of a conference room in which he had made a video presentation, he overheard one of the doctors say . . . 'You know, that old maverick nearly had me convinced.'

How does it work? Sunburn, as Dr Dabnly explains, is a slow-reacting bodymind response to the stimulus of excessive exposure to solar radiation and it takes about two hours to make itself felt. This allows ample time to provide suggestions to separate the stimulus and the response, in effect, to advise the control system that the overexposure has now ceased and that there is no need for the system to take belated protective action in the form of pumping liquid to inflate, irritate and blister the skin, or burn signals to remind you to get out of the sun.

Which, in turn, raises the question whether you can lie out in the sun all day long on your first day in Benidorm or relax on a bed of rusty nails and the answer is yes, if you set your mind to it. The benefit of being an analyst is that you may be reminded to pause for a moment to ponder what idiot thought-pattern is motivating your choice.

*   *   *

On the subject of cancer research, the BMA announced in 1991 that a research programme would be initiated to establish if cancer is a genetic problem or an environmental one, a programme similar to one already being carried out in Scotland. Apparently it is difficult to recognise ill-health simply as a living problem and therefore subject to mainly physical, mental, emotional, chemical and environmental influences, with parental neuroses and psychic influences playing a part.

I can accept that shedding my own scoliosis and spinal cancer with a simply hypnotic process after thirty years of orthodox treatment for the former and four for the latter could have been coincidental. But, luckily for me and for countless others, the hypnoanalytical process continues to work fast and can probably be further simplified and accelerated.

A criticism levied at all forms of 'alternative' healing methods is that they are unscientific. Yet, according to the British Medical Journal, only about fifteen-percent of medical treatments are supported by solid scientific evidence and only one-percent of the articles in medical journals is scientifically sound.

One of my clients, referred to elsewhere, came for therapy in the hope of avoiding the need for a sixth breast cancer operation. In cases like this, it is as well to forget that the medical approach to breast cancer operations has vacillated over the last hundred years from no treatment to mutilation and then back again to less drastic measures, without affecting mortality. The radical mastectomy operation, involving removal of the breast, the chest wall and the lymph nodes was developed over a hundred years ago. Longevity apart, it clearly does nothing for the quality of life.

Dr Bernie Siegel has done valiant service in striving to awaken doctrinaire minds at least to the need to watch their semantics, even when a patient is apparently asleep or anaesthetised.

The voice of authority impacts hard on the psyche of an emotionally vulnerable client and anyone seeking medical aid is certainly emotionally vulnerable. The most damaging impact of negative pronouncements ('Fat chance that leg will come good') is often revealed, in analysis, to have been caused by asides between a doctor and an assistant that they were unaware could be overheard or understood.

The following extract from a syndicated column by Dr Paul Solomon in the USA must have prompted Lottie to think 'sorry I asked':

Dear Dr Solomon: I have a breast lump that my doctor tells me is benign. But I'm concerned that it could become malignant. How often does something like this happen? – Lottie, Portland, Maine.

Dear Lottie: A benign breast lump does not become malignant. However, it is possible for a cancerous lump to develop near a benign lump.

A place for therapists to bear this point of negative conditioning firmly in mind is underlined by Prof Dr Max Lüscher in the introduction to the Lüscher test. For the therapist's information, occasional references are made in the text to negative possibilities. Clearly, no useful purpose is served in conveying them to a client or in allowing them to distract you from initiating the full healing process.

CONSCIOUS AFFIRMATIONS . . . WISHING MAKES IT SO?

It is still customary in some junior schools of hypnotherapy to provide clients with a list of potted affirmations or 'new thought patterns' to deal with a long list of diseases that most people are unaware exist. The list is presumably intended to provide some kind of hope to the hopeless and to be hidden from hypochondriacs. In easier times (pre-TV) Coué's famous affirmation was seemingly enough:
'Every day, in every way, I'm kidding myself that I'm getting better and better'. The catch with more specific forms of auto-suggestion is that the focus of conscious attention can serve to aggravate or reinforce the sensitivity that is creating a particular symptom, or even trigger a new one.
Like our commercialised tribal myths and fairy tales, belief in the power of auto-suggestion only adds to the world of fantasy and self-delusion from which it seems healthier to escape.
New thought patterns or affirmations would be effective if we could apply conscious thought patterns to change our subconscious conditioning, in the same way that it would be fun if we could levitate by tugging upwards on our own shoelaces.
The following is a verbatim extract from a letter from a new tape client, a yogist, which is illustrative of hundreds:

I am sorry for taking so long to return your colour test but I had a bad relapse. Although I started to feel better a few days ago I'm afraid I became very down once more. Before I had this relapse I had been feeling very positive even though my life is far from normal. Yet once again it really brought me down because I feel, no matter how determined, how positive I am, it always returns. When I try to concentrate on any positive affirmations, they are just empty words with no meaning. I can find no comfort in anything.

Then, this beauty:

I always believed in the power of the mind and told myself that if ever I became very ill I would get over it by positive thinking. Being so ill is my worst nightmare.'

The Lüscher results, in the case of this forty-year-old, were 5 2 3 4 1 0 6 7 and 2 4 3 0 5 1 7 6, as she started the process of throwing off the manipulative gameplaying that perhaps contributed to her 'myelodisplastic syndrome'.

"What's new?' is always recommended as a greeting for professional sufferers, as: 'How are we today?' invites a sorry tale. An alternative would be: 'How are we not today . . . not so good or not so bad?'

BIRTH AND PERINATAL EXPERIENCE IN THERAPY

As a reversal of the usual process, it was only after receiving reports from other hypnoanalysts of the results of using the Pilgrim 'Rebirthing' tape that I experimented with introducing a shortened version in face-to-face therapy. The results were surprisingly good and I felt proud that I had made a unique breakthrough. Some months later, I read that Dr David Cheek, MD, in the USA, had made the same discovery forty years ago.

Whether the client responds dramatically to the 'rebirthing' experience or not is unimportant. Access to the mental/emotional healing channels is invariably accelerated. This, in turn, facilitates identification of the birth or prenatal influences by working back, at a later stage in the session, from some compounding event that has been brought to consciousness. It soon becomes clear with effective hypnoanalysis, that most if not all of our major sensitivies are seeded in the womb. Consequently, it may prove worthwhile to develop a more elaborate script than the one provided in Prompt Sheet 19.

Roughly twenty-percent of my therapy clients are therapists or medical professionals. Most of them and many of my other clients have been to other hypnoanalysts or psychoanalysts and psychia- trists. One doctor had spent £2,000 on hypnoanalysis, another £10,000 on psychiatry. A lady analyst had been to five hypnoanalysts. An- other had endured four years of counselling, twice a week. In all these cases, the short rebirthing script produced the desired results.

The indications are, in these cases and most of the cases reported in books or provided for illustration in training courses in hypno- therapy, that the initial sensitising event has been mistakenly iden- tified (in the Freudian tradition) as occurring at the age of three or four or even later in life.

Consequently, the roots of the problem remain deeply buried in the prenatal stages of development, undisturbed and free to sprout again a few months after seemingly completing analysis. The effect is similar to dead-heading weeds in a garden. The garden looks good for a while.

John-Richard and Troye Turner, co-directors of the Institute for Whole-Self Discovery in Holland, have identified twenty-two spe- cific moments during gestation when emotional patterns are im- printed in the consciousness of the infant-to-be and can be identified to behavioural patterns later in life. Over ten-thousand cases are on record of clients who meaningfully experienced significant prenatal and perinatal sources of unwelcome behavioural patterns and were fully freed from them.

* * *

The following letter provides an example of a fairly heavy birthing experience:

> I have been introduced to you by (Analyst) who thinks you might be able to assist with my son's behaviour.
>
> My son, . . ., who was five on March 19, is having a lot of behavioural problems and getting into trouble at school. Whilst recently at the hospital, the staff mentioned that they thought him hyperactive. He has sessions of sudden screaming and shouting for about 10–15 minutes, then calms down again. He often will totally ignore anything you tell him and will scream or sing while you are trying to speak to him. He does not have many friends at school due to his behaviour and since Christ-

mas has been in trouble for fighting, throwing stones and hitting children with knives and forks; this is obviously not making him very popular.

On the occasions he is behaving well, he is quiet, very loving and polite and fairly insecure. He can basically be either angelic or horrific, no in-betweens. He has always been a little mischievous and very lively but this changed about the middle of last year and has got worse since. He has recently taken to going into our bedrooms and cutting curtains and painting the furniture after promising never to go into other people's rooms without permission again.

. . . has suggested giving you as many details as possible as this assists with preparing the right tape. He was a forceps delivery after being two weeks late and in distress; he had stopped moving two weeks before and at birth was having problems with his breathing and ended up with an infection, a drip in his arm and a week in the Intensive Care Department in an incubator. Last year, he had a general anaesthetic to remove a Lego man's hand from his nose and a couple of weeks ago another one to remove Play Doh from his ears. We also moved house in 1991 and again in 1992. He finished full-time nursery in July 1992 and started school in September 1992. Unfortunately no-one from his nursery went to the same school as him as we had moved by then. We have still stayed in – but there have been quite a few changes. He has been slightly asthmatic in the past, mostly at night and suffers from eczema, which was severe when he was younger but has improved considerably. Any colds and coughs he gets go straight to his chest and often make him sick.

We have tried cutting out different foods but this hasn't helped at all. Is there anything you can do before he gets expelled from school or his father or I throttle him?

The young lad's Lüscher test results read: 7 4 1 2 0 3 5 6 / 4 5 3 7 1 2 6 0, clearly confirming the sad story in numbers, particularly the mood swings from self-destructive behaviour to over-excitement and childish fantasies. The improvement in the second choice and the relatively low level of stress provided some unexpected leeway in preparing a special whisper subliminal tape. This and the Pilgrim 'Child Self-Esteem' tapes had the desired effect of helping the hypnotherapist to work effectively with the young lad in therapy. The parents also provided their Lüscher selections and accepted my tape recommendations.

Professor Dr Fedor-Freyberg of Stockholm and of the International Society of Perinatal and Preinatal Psychology and Medicine provides this thought: 'The prenatal stage of life is that period where primary prevention needs to be practised, where early disturbances are to be avoided, where prenatal and perinatal morbidity and mortality can be reduced, where a decent start to life can be given and, finally, where the fundamental humanitarian values through early bonding of child and mother and father can be facilitated.'

Accepting that our 'genetic encoding' or emotionally-conditioned DNA are thought patterns that have been seeded in the womb, creating at least our major sensitivies, the next question is: which womb? The ancient Zen theme is that the education of a child starts a thousand years before its parents are born. We learn now that some six million or so fertilisable eggs are formed in the womb of every five-week-old female embryo and the fact that they are influenced by emotive thought processes is not just part of my own experience in working with panic-attack cases in analysis. So it becomes conceivable that this is the link to 'previous life experiences'. Many of these arise quite spontaneously in therapy, often with clients who have neither the education nor the imagination to write a short story. Yet the events are described in such detail that they are uncomfortably real to me and clearly prove to have a therapeutic effect on the client.

So perhaps it is not surprising to learn that, having broken down 'matter' to the smallest perceptible element, the best description that science can offer to the 'solid' part is that, in its behaviour, it resembles a thought-form.

* * *

PURPOSE OF THERAPY   We are going to initiate a process, you and I, to make something happen that will be of immense benefit to you . . . something that will bring a great quality and intensity of experience back to your lifestyle . . . and to do so as you creatively relax.

LOG-JAM RELEASE   Your sensitivities have created an emotional log-jam which has to be released . . . but we don't have to lift any logs . . . it's not as difficult a job as that. We just have to ask subcon to redirect the energy that put the logs there in the first place . . . to allow the negative energy to vent.

LOVE ATTACHMENT   The neurotic love contract? 'You will love me and only me every moment of your life and you will never love anyone else as much . . . and I will love you in the same way.' Loving is not a relationship . . . it is a state of being and subject to continuous change and renewal. It is the deepest form of human understanding. Your depth of lovingness is measured by the feelings you have for the people closest to you, loving them more strongly than others because you know them better . . . you understand their weaknesses as well as their strengths, loving them even though they are unable to respond in kind. Loving in the same way that a rose perfumes the air around it. If the loving is shared, it's a bonus, a benediction . . . never a need. (If you seek to become attached, attach yourself to an icecream cone).

CAN'T BE HELPED   You say you have tried everything and everybody and that you feel that you just can't be helped. What does that tell you about yourself? What it tells me is that you feel that you are not worthy of help. Let's find if that's true and where that feeling is centred.

LIFE DRAGS   You find life has become a drag? Perhaps you need thoughts you can live with. Let's start with one that you need to dump. Pick one that really drags heavily on you. Let's find what resource you need to overcome it.

PURPOSE IN LIFE   Your purpose in life is to enjoy it. You can treat it as a dress rehearsal for something else or decide to focus on living, **every new moment of now**. The more energy you direct to making a living the less is going into learning how to live with yourself. You are a process of continuous change and renewal. Keep mental and emotional pace with it.

CREATIVE RELAXATION   When you relax creatively your awareness in creases by more than three thousand per cent. Sit . . . and find out for yourself.

DEPRESSION RELEASE | Further repressions will release gently through the natural medium of dreams and experiences at times when it is safe and appropriate for subcon to order their release to consciousness.

ACCEPTANCE | Subcon will only accept and implement my suggestions and observations to the extent that they are appropriate to your needs and beneficial in promoting your vibrant good health and wellbeing.

NEED | Is there any level of mind or being that still feels the need to hold on to some repressed emotion or self-limiting negative belief-pattern? Is there anything else we need to know at the so-called conscious levels to be entirely free of the problem?

YES OR NO | Please respond quickly 'yes' or 'no' – do you want to be relieved of the problem?

PAIN REMOVAL | Your subconscious controls removed the pain because you accepted my suggestions . . . now subcon will respond to your suggestions. I will ask subcon to induce the feeling . . . you will immediately turn it off – just tense and relax a hand and mentally say: 'Pain -go!'

SUBCON CORRECT | Can subcon make all the necessary corrections without the need to bring further details to consciousness? Are there physical influences still to be released? There's the person (proffer a heavy cushion) – what do you want to do to him/her?

SELF-HYPNOSIS | Conscious self-hypnosis is a state of enhanced awareness, it's a knack. Get it right once, you need no further guidance.

ABREACTION | Regress to an event, change tense to present tense. 'Intensify the emotion, clarify the picture at the count of three.'

AWARENESS | The client's enhanced awareness conveys to you and leads you to the healing. Be prepared to change direction. The cause of a problem is just below the surface of consciousness awaiting an opportunity to vent.

TRANSFERENCE

What conveys to others is what you are in your thoughts most of the time.

WITNESS STATE

With every breath that you take your awareness increases and you can go back and relive any event in your life as a witness and re-experience it from the perspective of a mature adult mind, you will see clearly what created the emotional impact . . . and the problem will cease to bother you once and for all.

NO RESPONSE

At the count of three, subcon will give you the response to that question and you will tell me . . . 1 2 3 (click). (You may need to rephrase the question you asked).

INDUCE FEELING

When is your problem at its worst? Now go to another event . . . let's see if the same influences are involved.

DREAMSTREAM

In a moment, an odd thing is going to happen. When I have you open your eyes, I will chat to you and you will see me touch my forehead and you will fall deeply asleep . . . you won't remember me giving you that suggestion but you will be precisely guided by it . . . I will repeat that ('you will see me' etc.) . . . and you will dream and the dreamstream will tell you exactly what happened and how the problem was caused and you will be able to tell me if it furthers the healing process . . . now, open your eyes . . . you feel very relaxed? . . . (touch your forehead). Allow time for the sleep state to develop. REM (rapid eye movement) will indicate dreamstream state. Quietly: 'You will respond to my questions but you will not wake up. (Repeat) Where are you now in your dream?'

ANAESTHESIA

Now watch . . . all I have to do is click my fingers and the anaesthesia will jump from your hand to the centre of discomfort . . . the discomfort will be completely relieved.

POSITIVE FOCUS   Relax, centre and focus mindpower on how you want to see things happen, not on what you seek to avoid . . . bring to mind an emotionalized picture of your success . . . it serves as an attracting force. At this vibrational level of reality called life, duality rules . . . every channel is a two-way channel. The success you are seeking is seeking you.

IMPOTENCE, FRIGIDITY   In therapy, you may sometimes find this is linked to an event that seeded a desire to die.

FINGER SIGNAL   Just relax and let it come clearly to consciousness and when you can talk to me about it your yes-finger will rise.

ALTERNATIVES   I will now ask subcon on your behalf and for the benefit of the entire bodymind system to provide a more immediate, a more appropriate and a more life-enhancing alternative to the part or parts or cells or functions that have been motivated to create a self-limiting symptom. Your yes-finger will rise as soon as subcon has initiated the healing actions and all functions of the bodymind system are responding appropriately. Subcon . . . are any further changes in thinking habits or behavioural patterns required?

ASS OF YOU AND ME   Never assume you have the answer. Ask subcon.
CLIENT ATTITUDE   Whatever the client's response or attitude . . . 'great' . . . and work on from there. Work well with what you get. Subcon forgives your mistakes but not your excuses. Your function is to initiate an effective process of change and then get your head out of the way.

DIRECT TO CAUSE   When I gently tap your forehead (in the area of the pineal gland) . . . a letter of the alphabet will spring to mind . . . the letters will spell a word . . . the word will direct you to the cause of the problem . . . there you are . . . quickly now . . . what's the first letter? The next letter . . . you know the word . . . what is the word? At the count of three, you will know what caused your problem . . . 1 2

3 . (The word may surface in the client's mother-tongue. Be prepared to ask for the meaning of the word in English).

GESTALT

You couldn't tell him then . . . you can tell him now. Put your father over there on a chair and tell him how you feel about him. Ask him, in your own words, did he understand anything about your needs as a child. Tell him what you didn't tell him then – give him back his anger . . . you've been carrying it deep down inside you far too long . . . let it go now.

HOME VISIT

When I raise and drop your arm you are back at home as a child on a Saturday or Sunday . . . tell me, who is there? How do you feel about them? What are they discussing?

SAFE HOUSE

For you, it is no longer just a choice between fight or flight. You have a safe house to function from . . . you will automatically be there in case of need and whenever you draw a long, slow, deep breath and allow your stomach to relax and expand . . . you will be guided to spontaneous right action.

SOFTLY SOFTLY

Allow silences for feelings to surface.

FIDGETS

Unless the sleep state is induced, young children may fidget continuously even though they are in deep hypnosis. They are still highly suggestible.

EMPATHY

As an experienced professional, you always start from strength, from authority, and you maintain it. Effective hypno-analysis is a win-win game. Your client improves in health and wellbeing. With each client, you improve as a therapist. Fail to do so . . . use the process to find out why.

MISDIRECTED ENERGY

When you push something unwelcome to the back of your mind, you provide energy to it, like trying to sink a beachball. A lot of life-energy can be misdirected to maintaining ill-health. It can be redirected to creative purpose.

ALFRED,
LORD TENNYSON

'Comes a vapour from the margin,
Blackening over heath and holt,
Cramming all the blast before it,
In its breast a thunderbolt.'
In brief, climatic abreaction.

FRED, ANALYST

'The main theme in hypnoanalysis is to encourage you to look more deeply into things with your eyes closed.'

FEES

The professional who attracts numerous clients despite charging high fees is not necessarily the most effective therapist. He is a professional who attracts numerous clients despite charging high fees.

LOVE

How do you attract a loving partner? By creating lots of love of life in yourself. Are you reaching for love, comfort, security outside yourself? Let's find out what introduced the need for it . . . what created unreasoned fears and insecurity.

EGO BOOSTING

Boosting the ego is not part of the healing process. The ego is part of the problem. By promoting deeper self-understanding, the false ego is by-passed, from within.

COMFORT

'Take off your shoes if that will make you feel more comfortable and relaxed.'

MODES OF ADDRESS

From a letter: 'To Mr Duncan McColl, FCA, MIAPT, MISPH. Dear Sir or Madam'.

Telephone: an urgent request for tape advice from a young single mother. To speed the plough, I asked her to list the eight Lüscher colours and make her selections. I then gave her a brief overview and recommended two tapes. The following night, a young friend of hers telephoned from the same Welsh town: 'Is Mr Duncan there, please . . . the man who does fortune-telling by phone?'

I was lucky enough to be introduced to hypnotherapy by a true mind-master who recognised that a minute's practical demonstration is worth more than a thousand words. Presenters at meetings and annual conferences are not in this class. A one-sentence thought becomes a sixty-minute harangue. An international convention in Houston in 1990 was no exception. Two of the first three speakers overran their allotted time by ten minutes and all three of them started with the same routine opener . . . 'It gives me very great pleasure to address such a distinguished international audience including our two colleagues from London, England.' The net result was that the chairman had to warn the next speaker that lunch was fixed for one o'clock so he asked her to be sure to keep her presentation short. The subject was 'Sex' . . . and she started in exactly the same way as the others with: 'Ladies and gentlemen, it gives me very great pleasure,' and then she sat down.

FORGIVE

What was your father trying to achieve by being stern with you? Perhaps he was doing his level best – within the limits of his conditioning of course – to prepare you to meet the kind of life-challenges that he had encountered. And your understanding is clearer now because he behaved that way. Can you forgive him for trying to do his best for you? Forgive – not necessarily excuse . . . and move on to greater things.

INSOMNIA

Insomnia is the denial of a basic human need so let's find the cause of the thoughts that keep you from relaxing into refreshing sleep. Somewhere in the past you had a significant emotional experience – some event or other that disturbed the natural sleeping pattern, and the influence is still there, expressing itself at some level below consciousness. How do you describe the feeling that you get when you seek to relax into sleep? Where – in the body – do you feel it? Let's ask subcon to bring on the feeling now . . . somewhere in the bodymind system . . . at the count of three.

VITAL STATISTICS

Fifty-trillion intelligent cells make up the bodymind system, which is ten thousand times more cells than the Earth's present population. They communicate through fourteen-billion neural connections, more than one-thousand times the number of telephone connections in the world. Each of the fifty-trillion cells can perform five-hundred or more functions. Twenty-four billion blood cells at the last count circulate throughout the body every fifteen seconds and four-hundred-million cells extract oxygen from each breath and unload carbon dioxide. The heart pumps thirty-five million times a year and, in fifty years, pumps forty-five million gallons of blood. A smoker's heart beats an extra three-million times a year, giving the heart about ten-percent more work. (Smoking is not the cause. Stress is). Ninety-eight-percent of the bodymind cells are renewed every year. Your skin is renewed every month, your skeleton every three, and you get a new stomach lining every four days.

PERFECTION

Perfection is not a human attribute. We can aspire to excellence. Be happy about that. Let the love of life blossom in you and save some of that love for yourself.

LAST GOODBYE

So – tell her now: it's never too late for love. Tell her goodbye . . . tell her you love her . . . tell her you understand . . . you will be all right . . . tell her in your own words. What does she say? Now let your mind become clear and notice how wonderful you feel . . . you now experience a deeper understanding of the eternal . . . of love.

PLAYTIME

'Right . . . put the skin problem on the chair over there and ask it what its creative purpose is . . . what good does it think it is doing for you or anyone else.' Gestalting, NLP, raja yoga and any similar 'show-biz' techniques can sometimes be introduced to provide light relief before initiating the more effective healing techniques.

POST-HYPNOTIC
SUGGESTION

Whenever you choose to relax creatively you can initiate the healing process yourself and you know that it will be fully effective.

LOOK INSIDE

Now go down to the area of the spine where the problem is manifesting and compare it with the healthy tissue around it . . . tell me . . . what do you see . . . the colour . . . the shape . . . the size. Now . . . bring the mental sunlight in and focus it on the problem area . . . feel it warm and glow and heal and heal and heal. Leave the light there . . . the light knows what to do . . . the bodymind system knows how to respond. Now . . . go forward three months in calendar time . . . at the count of three . . . one . . . two . . . three. There you' are: now look inside . . . tell me . . . what do you see. (Then go forward five years).

BLAME

In relationship problems, no one person is ever to blame. If you must seek something to blame, blame the relationship, then see what options you have to change it.

RELAXATION

I am going to raise your arm and leave it raised . . . and as you feel the discomfort increase let it return slowly to your lap and as it goes down, feel the relaxation increase so that when it touches your lap you will be ten times more deeply relaxed . . . slowly now . . . allow it to lower only as fast as you feel the relaxation increase and spread to every nerve and cell and system of the body.

SCIENCE

The scientific or logical mind is a conditioned mind . . . a linear-conditioned mind. It has difficulty in living without neat answers. Life is seen, for example, as a continuous process of change and renewal, but logically, of course, it must have a beginning and an end. The 'Big Bang Theory' is in vogue at the moment, to explain how the Universe began. First there was nothing, then it exploded. Our conditioning hides the obvious from us. Alan Watts simplified it for us by suggesting that, in responding to the question, which came first, the bird or the egg, that a bird is just an egg's way of laying more eggs. A planet is just a star's way of having more stars. If you cease to deal in shallow-minded opposites like 'ordinary' and 'enlightened', illusion will cease of itself. Every moment of life is significant if you accept each experience as leading you onwards in a spirit of adventure into the unknown.

ALL CHANGE

If a process of change, once initiated, takes time or effort, the process needs to be changed. Change is ineffective unless it conveys to all aspects of mind and being instantaneously. It invokes a spontaneous realisation, not a linear process of thought. It can happen or be caused when the climate is right. The experiential or dualistic level of reality is only one of the levels available to us and if we lose contact with the other levels, it is the level on which we find ourselves most fallible. As long as we are locked into our thoughts, we are functioning from the superficial, linear-restricted levels of mind, from our past conditioning. We are separated from ongoing living reality, because living is not a linear process. So . . . we need to be more spiritually oriented, perhaps? This, again, is neither a 'holy' nor a 'whole' state of mind. It invokes the same shallow-minded concept of duality, of good and bad, saint and sinner, god and devil . . . the same conceptual error that separates man from man and man from Nature. It is our failure to appreciate that 'opposites' are manifestations or degrees of the same thing . . . 'hot' just means less cold and 'cold' means less hot. Thankfully, practically anyone can learn to use conscious self-hypnosis effectively to distinguish between self-understanding and self-delusion. However, as any effective analytical hypnotherapist appreciates, there are aspects of self-hypnosis that it is unwise to convey verbally or in writing. Like the secrets of success, they can best be entrusted to someone capable of accepting the responsibility. Understanding alone is not enough unless it leads us to noble purpose. Tapping into the creative and healing channels day by day, it soon becomes apparent that self-understanding is not just a matter of life and death. It is much more important than that.

SESSION CHECK-SHEET
(Aide-memoir)

Elman fast induction . . . respond to phase one, phase two. Fix finger, eyes open, ensure finger stays rigid, eyes close, relax.

Turn off any minor distractions temporarily (coughing, tinnitus, etc).

Phase three basement . . . sub-basement, through zero.

Tap forehead, word to link to major problem.

Put the word in a sentence.

Feeling produced. Where? Back to the first time.

Check with ideodynamics.

Dream 60 seconds (time-out for analyst).

Birth-experience.

Ego-state, speak to part 'X'. Seek the creative purpose.

Trace name on hand, erase. Memory bypassed?

Thumb movement to advise discomfort.

Compound: back to school, first walk, first holiday/picnic.

Subcon provide a word for the primary feeling.

Visualisation? Telephone, tree, orange. The word conveys.

Ten, wide awake. Zero, deeply relaxed. Where on the ruler are you?

Colour of ruler? Colour of numbers on the ruler?

Recheck arms for relaxation.

Children, induce sleep state if necessary.

Ideodynamics . . . 'put into words before the finger moves'.

Symbol of major problem area will appear.

Enhanced coping skills . . . anchor to a successful event.

Previous life experience.

Swish pattern . . . picture new pattern replacing the old one.

Future pace . . . test power of the anchor to override problems.

Pinpointing: did you have the problem at age ten? Five? Etc.

Go to 15 minutes before the event that created the sensitivity.

Go through the event as a witness . . .put it on a video screen.

Verify all parts benefiting, symptom no longer required.

See yourself having the dream – you will see the meaning.

From zero to ten, where do you stand on the four fundamental life needs?

Forest trip – person who hurt you.

Forgive, not necessarily excuse. How could they overcome their conditioning? (By analysis).

What secondary benefits were being offered to you as bait?

Ideal body image.

Deep relaxation, phase X – forward 30, 40 years.

Talents – in touch with inner guide.

Reluctance to disclose: 'Anything bothering you?'

Can you reveal your feelings to me in say – three years time?

Future pace three years.

Touch forehead: a word springs to mind to link to the cause of the problem.

Emotions, jealousy, etc. Feel nothing? 'Let's see if subcon agrees.' (Thumb waggle).

'I see nothing' . . . because . . . finish the sentence.

I'll raise and drop your arm . . . you'll finish the sentence.

You feel different . . . because . . .?

Timeline process to eliminate guilt, etc.

Subcon will bring to mind your best resources.

Your index finger will rise to let me know you see your resources, one by one.

Hand-raised process to deal with problem.

Now . . . your three best options.

Subcon will select the best.

Take forward five years, to see results.

Personality type . . . paint a verbal picture of the polar opposites. Merge them.

Habit pattern – what triggered the initial reaction?

Gestalt: put your father over there, tell him how you feel.

There he is (offer heavy cushion). What do you want to do to him?

Lack of self-worth . . . where do you feel it?

Internal check . . . healthy / unhealthy tissue . . . future pace.

Demonstrate self-induced anaesthesia if required.

Light to any area of discomfort or concern, change vibrations automatically.

Anchor to love, success, holiday feeling.

Multiply feelings.

Whose standards have you been seeking to meet?

Do other people meet yours?

Whose thinking patterns have you been entertaining?

Do you need them now?

The 'awakening' – clear out past conditioning.

Any other problem to resolve now?

Causal factor . . . influence of compounding factors . . . all clear?

What changes in behavioural patterns required: subcon will convey now.

Go seven days ahead, review influence of analysis.

Thank subcon.

You do better than well – you excel.

Any fun-time you would like to relive?

Any comment you would like to make on our work?

Take five . . . and see if there is anything you need to ask me or tell me.

Now take five and see if you have a question for subcon.

Attenuate heavy experiences . . . emotions all released mentally, emotionally, physically? Link to keyword.

Return to 'everyday living reality' . . . test access to control levels.

Test anchors . . . success, love, holiday feeling.

Tell me . . . do you do better than well?

('I excel'). Can't hear you . . . convince me . . . do you do better than well?

How do you feel about knowing yourself better?

That's a word . . . I asked . . . how do you **feel? Show me!**

SIX EASY STEPS TO STRESS RELIEF

SIT . . . and take five for yourself three times a day. Fifteen minutes a day for yourself – for yourself, not for your thoughts. Let thoughts come and go. Focus on the spaces in between. Intuition is born there.

RELAX . . . CREATIVELY. You can drop down to a lower level of tension and fail to relax. Thoughts are the barrier. Take one or two conscious breaths. Do it now, focusing each time on the outgoing breath. You have just telegraphed your treasurehouse mind that you want to relax, creatively. As you inhale again, allow your stomach to relax and expand. Expanding your stomach, you override the startle pattern you inherited as a child.

STIMULATE AWARENESS. Allow one of your hands to dangle down by your side. Become aware of the tingling sensation at the fingertips. Notice how your general awareness expands as you cease to be lost in your thoughts and begin to come to your senses . . . to your bodymind sensing system. Go to your fingers from time to time and sense the natural rhythm and flow in the work that you do. When you go with the flow, work becomes a joy. You learn to work smarter rather than harder.

GO TO YOUR MOUTH . . . and turn the corners down as far as you can. Frown, and hold the frown for a few seconds or so. NOW . . . switch to a smile. Notice the difference in how you feel. Make smiling a habit. Whenever. There is magic, powerful magic, in your smile.

LINK TO HAPPINESS. Focus on a time and a place or a person, a time when everything went just right for you. A big success! Select a keyword that will always bring the occasion to mind in the future. As you bring on the feeling of success again, make a fist, repeat the keyword . . . and relax. Mental, emotional, sensory mindset. From now onwards, whenever you clench your fist and mentally repeat the cue-word, you will induce the feeling of success. At the deeper levels of mindpower, like attracts like. This way, if the facts in your life are unfriendly . . . you can change the facts.

USE THE PROCESS. Practise it, enjoy it. Whatever you do con-sciously with feeling a few times becomes a habit . . . a conditioned reflex . . . in this case, a healthy habit. The concepts are not new. They were recognised by Hermes Trismegistus, the Master of Mas-ters, about five thousand years ago. They are the initial steps on a journey to inner space.

Time now to take five.

Friends in High Places

How do you convince people who function exclusively from their heads that they function more effectively if they also listen to their hearts?

As a healer-therapist, you know the answer. Unless people have a compelling need to know, their heads will tend to stand in their way.

Take a case of a client who has been handicapped by a spinal injury for thirty years. He has sought the best orthodox advice available in several countries. He has also been warned authoritatively that the *scoliosis* could develop into cancer and he has dutifully converted this negative conditioning into reality, contributing *degenerative bone tissue* for good measure. He now has the urgent need to know if he can avoid submitting to a knife.

In precision therapy, his long-felt need ensures that he is a fully responsive client. Within an hour, he experiences a strong physical, mental and emotional indication that healing has been initiated. 'Why,' he asks, 'doesn't everyone know about this process?'

Healers have been active worldwide for at least thousands of years. Good books have been written about them. The catch is that the books are not only outdated before they are written, the teachings are largely unintelligible because they are largely personal. As in those moments in therapy when the conditioning fades and the spirit soars, the words of the masters were conveyed spontaneously on a one-to-one basis, addressing the precise needs of the moment. Essentially, they reflect the inner sense of receptivity of the listener. The greater the need, the greater the receptivity. The relevance, the significance and the beneficial impact are all in the mood of the moment, not just in the choice of words. The head is only used to initiate process. Healing starts when the heart calls the play.

We can generally accept that life-energy, in some form or other, permeates everything, everyone, everywhere all of the time . . . a manifestation, if you like, of creative exuberance, an energy-field that is neither kind nor unkind. We limit perception of our own participation if we personify the power in any way. Partially con-

232

scious of our peripheral senses of sight, sound, taste, touch and smell, we lose touch with the creative sensory system that develops and maintains us. Like electricity, unseen, it is a power to direct, to use or abuse. Once released from the constraints of self-limiting negative conditioning, our extrasensory powers are free to provide the healing required.

All good stuff, of course, but this still does not explain why so many people fail to appreciate their healing powers. Simplification of one of the earliest teachings can provide a clue, if we limit consideration to seven fairly understandable levels of being, with physical development as *number one*, as we evolve from pure consciousness to form . . . we 'arrive'.

Phase two : emotional and sexual awareness, body consciousness. We develop basic sensory perception.

Phase three: intellectual development. We think, we react. At the top end of this scale, we aspire to better ourselves with brainpower, to become professionals, politicians, religious leaders etc. Emphasis is on ego, willpower and a good standard of living.

Four: psychic awareness. We feel, we act. Awareness expands, supplanting willpower, promoting deeper sensory perception, insight, intuition, spontaneity of right action. Emphasis is on quality of life.

Five : transcendental stage. Precognitionary skills expand. Wisdom replaces fear and ego.

Six: bliss state. Overcome doubt.

Seven: enlightenment. Overcome bliss.

Phase three is limited to beliefs . . . to faith, the lazy mind's excuse for not seeking truth. Initiation to level four is usually achieved with difficulty and with a pronounced shift in the bodymind system, a bitter-sweet impact sometimes identified as the 'AH-HA' moment. Generations of self-limiting negative conditioning are spontaneously cleared.

Paradoxically, the more 'advanced' the intellectual or doctrinaire mind in level three, the less likely the quantum leap to self-understanding. This is where the impetus of a traumatic experience or life-threatening event is usually required. The herd-mind is heavily conditioned and easily misled by the minor masters and mystics who flutter for a while in the limelight in the lower reaches of phase four, impelled by a neurotic urge to attract followers.

So the game of life will continue to be played out at all levels. Effective healing guidance will continue to be found by those who are strongly motivated to seek. The aggressor and the exploiter will continue to flourish, driven by fear and greed and ignorance. Votes will continue to be counted rather than weighed and the meek will inherit the earth, but not the mineral rights. The wise will avoid nursing despondenccy or indulging in worry, appreciating that Earth is a minor planet anyway. The few genuine inverse paranoids will continue to explore and enjoy life to the full, avoiding things that leave a nasty taste in the mind, secure in the knowledge that life at its best calls out to everyone . . . a thought that is always worth keeping firmly in mind.

BIBLIOGRAPHY

A Complete Guide to Therapy, Joel Kovel (Penguin).

Caduceus Journal, 38 Russell Terrace, Leamington Spa, Warwickshire, CV31 1HE (monthly).

Frogs into Princes, Richard Bandler & John Grinder (Real People Press).

Hypnotherapy, Dave Elman (Westwood Publishing).

Love, Medicine and Miracles, Bernie Siegal (Anchor Brendon).

Mind-Body Therapy, Rossie & Cheek (W.W. Norton & Co.)

Quantum Healing, Deepak Chopra (Bantam).

The Lüscher Colour Test (Washington Square Press) (Tao of Books).

The Mustard Seed, Osho (Tao of Books, 7 Willow Farm, Allwood Green, Rickinghall, Diss IP22 1LT).

The Zen Manifesto, Osho (as above).

Transforming Therapy, Gil Boyne (Westwood Publishing).

Trauma, Trance & Transformation, M. Gerald Edelstein (Brunner Mazel).

What Doctors Don't Tell You (WDDTY), 4 Wallace Road, London, N1 2PG (bi-monthly).

INDEX

Abreaction 133
acceptance 14, 217
acrophobia 126
affection 65
affirmations 211–2
age regression 71
anaesthesia 218
analyst's function 15
anchor 127
anger 75
anorexia 125
anxiety 76
assertiveness 60
assumption 219
asthma 126
attenuation 65
attitude 219
avoidance 76
awakening 87
awareness 47, 105, 217–8

Barrier state 131
basement level 38, 95
beliefs 95, 122–3, 211
biofeedback 122
birth 49, 128, 131, 133, 136, 137, 183, 185, 212–15
birthright 15
blame 224
body image 103
brain damage 122
bypass critical 99

Cancer 111, 126, 128, 129, 159, 192, 205–11
carers 159
case history 111, 125
causative event 71
challenge 121
change 225

change emotions 75
check-sheet 227
chemotherapy 122
childhood 76
children 24, 196, 230
choices 15
click fingers 97
closing 24–5
coma 127, 133, 192
compounding 22–23
conception 137
conditional reflex 96
conditioning 67, 122–3
confidence 121
confusion 44–5
conscious self-hypnosis 15
coping skills 54–5, 94
creative relaxation 37–38, 45, 216
critical faculty 99

Death 135
deepening 22, 37–8, 44, 59, 93
depression 90, 127
diabetes 126, 129
discomfort 140
divorce 129
double-checking 48
doubt 98, 132
dream 47, 140, 196, 218
duality 123, 225

Earlier life 77
ego-boosting 221
ego-state 43, 63, 92, 139
Elman 37, 46, 69, 88, 100
emotions 65, 75, 215
energy 61–2
enhanced coping 54–55
Esdaile state 38, 133, 188
euphoria 129, 136

expectations 97

Feelings 33–34, 39, 56
fees 221
fertility 186–7
finger signals 120, 219
forest trip 73
forgiveness 51, 67, 222
foundling child 129
frigidity 219
fundamental needs 60
future pace 53, 106

Game change 123
gestalt 71, 220
goodbye 223
guilt 76, 81

Habit change 91
homosexual 129, 136
hope 60
hurt 73
hypnosis 225

Ideomotor response 43, 48, 92, 120,
    134
impotence 219
improve 84
induce feelings 56
induction 26, 27, 32, 35
infancy 71, 118
initial sensitising 31, 66, 213
initiate process 15, 68
insomnia 222
instant pain-relief 102
internal 85
introduction 13

Jealousy 76, 95, 127

Keywords 121

Levels I, II, III 37–8
lifeforce 119
life needs 60, 98, 118, 216
lifestyle 15
link, connect 39, 76
lock mind 14
lonely 96–7
love 121, 216, 221

Lüscher test 134, 155–60, 196, 211,
    212, 214, 221

Mastersheet 18
malignancy 119
manic depressive 125
medical coma 127, 192
medical tests 122
memory 30
mental retention 32
molester 126
monkey mind 33

Nature 119
negative conditioning 122
negative responses 40–42
neo-Freudians 198
nothing 40, 41, 42, 106
nothingness 14
numbers 70

Objective 15, 82, 93
one energy 13
options 106, 121, 125, 131, 141

Pain relief 102, 142, 217
panic attack 94, 129
parents 188
perfectionism 76, 97, 223
performance 84
phase II 36
phase X 85
phobia 89, 129
pinpointing 46
playacting 76
positive focus 15, 219
possessiveness 76
post-operation 134–5
powerhouse mind 15
prebirth 77
precision therapy 33, 143
predicates 98
presenting problem 38
previous life 77, 127, 143
private therapy 57–8
problems 104
process 68
prompt sheet 19
psychic energies 14
psychosclerosis 98

Question time 139
question responses 145
quotations 196

Raja-yoga 122
rationale 13, 19
redirection 61
regression 143
relationship 107, 134
relaxation 14, 37, 69, 72, 93, 111, 124
reluctance 53
reminders 92
repressions 96
resistance 13
resources 44
respect 60

Safe house 220
schizophrenia 159
school 96
science 224
seal break 88, 100, 132, 135
self-confidence 121, 128
self-worth 94
sensing system 14
sensitivity 33, 126, 213
seriously ill 13
session check-sheet 227
shame 81
sharing 123
silences 220
skills 83
skin problem 223
sleep state 30, 137

slow responses 79
solutions 104
spontaneous remission 97
spontaneous right action 15
stress 191–2
stroke 134
sub-basement 95
subliminals 182
success 60, 82, 121, 133
suggestibility 88
suggestions 52
suicide 125, 131, 194

Talents 80
taped therapy 134–5, 161, 175–198
tap head 39
test, change 48
test for relaxation 15
therapy introduction 16
therapy mastersheet 18–19
therapy purpose 215
thumb waggle 66
tinnitus 125, 132
tumours 119

uncovering 20
unrelaxed 52

Vital statistics 223

Water phobia 128
weight problem 126
worthy 94
wounded child-mind 51

Zero state 59

Precision Analysis Case

"Friday the 17th April 1987 was the date when I had a fully loaded nine-millimetre pistol aimed at my head and the trigger was pulled. Fortunately, my would-be murderer was so drunk that he had not slipped the safety-catch or I would not be here to write this. The strange thing, with hindsight, was the lack of immediate reaction on my part. I was leading a very active life serving with a Special Forces unit at the time and violent, often bloody, incidents were not rare. It wasn't until a number of years later, by which time I was firmly settled back into civilian life, that this incident began to plague me. I began to have flashbacks, nightmares, anxieties and full-blown panic attacks. My temper became instant and dangerous, on more than one occasion literally seeing red and terrifying any members of the general population who happened to be in the area. I also became very depressed and began to think that maybe it was time to end it all.

By the time I discovered Precision Therapy I had already been to a counsellor, a psychologist and three hypnotherapists of various schools. Their competence in their own individual areas of expertise was obvious, but none of them was able to offer any worthwhile assistance apart from diagnosing Post Traumatic Stress Disorder. They were able to wax lyrical about the theory (having read about it) but I did not wish to be anyone's experiment while they employed the 'try this and try that' approach. None of them appreciated that certain PTSD sufferers do not respond well to prolonged intervention systems. In all cases certain parts of my experience were over-emphasised while others were ignored or played down. It was also disconcerting for me, as a client, to pick up the panic signals two of these therapists exhibited when things failed to go as planned.

I attended my Precision Therapy session hopeful, but not knowing what to expect. In any case, this was going to be the last throw of the dice - I'd had enough! Within 60 short minutes I had my life back. Another 60 short minutes returned my optimism and sense of humour! Lingering issues were addressed and again successfully dealt with in one session by a second Precision-trained therapist about a year later. The power of Precision Therapy for me turned out to be the precise (pun not intended) nature of the intervention. My own conception of what to expect from a therapy situation, and my inherent resistances were neatly side-stepped by the therapist going straight to the crux of the matter.

That was all several years ago and I'm still going strong in a challenging job without the need for any further therapy".

The Magic of Mind Power: Awareness Techniques for the Creative Mind
Duncan McColl

Drawing together threads from hypnotherapy, behavioural science, Zen, Sufism and esoteric Christianity, Duncan McColl weaves them into a practical self-help guide to the immense potential of the human mind. Using visualisation, creative imagery and self-hypnosis, he provides a fresh perspective on developing personal skills to eliminate negative conditioning which produces ill-health, lack of energy and low self-esteem. Cutting through the usual aura of mystery which surrounds hypnotic practices, the straightforward, informative and authoritative style of this book makes it *the ideal way to unlock creativity and discover the magic of mind power.*

Paperback   **192 pages**   **ISBN** 1899836292

Ericksonian Approaches: A Comprehensive Manual
Rubin Battino MS & Thomas L. South PhD

A highly acclaimed, outstanding training manual in the art of Ericksonian hypnotherapy. Accessible and elucidating, it provides a systematic approach to learning set against a clinical background, developing the reader's learning over twenty-two chapters which include: the history of hypnosis; myths and misconceptions; rapport-building skills; language forms; basic and advanced inductions; utilisation of ideodynamic responses; basic and advanced metaphor and Ericksonian approaches in medicine, dentistry, substance abuse and life-challenging diseases.

"This book should undoubtedly be read and re-read by any who consider themselves to be hypnotherapists. But it should not be limited to them. If people who are not interested in the subject of hypnotherapy are not drawn to it, this will be a loss for anyone who uses language in the course of therapeutic work ... I highly recommend this book." – *Barry Winbolt, The New Therapist.*

Hardback   **564 pages**   **ISBN** 1899836314

Also available: a companion audiotape of Exercises and Demonstrations – 65 mins. **ISBN** 189983642X

Coping: A Practical Compendium for People with Life-Challenging Diseases and their Caregivers
Rubin Battino MS

How do you cope with a life-challenging disease? How you respond can have a profound effect on the physical course of the illness. There is a healing power in hope, and a destructive power in despair. Attitude matters. Some people seem to be 'naturally' better at creating the right attitude, but we can all learn to improve our coping skills.

Coping is a practical compendium for those living with or dealing with life-challenging diseases. Detailing the many effective coping strategies that Professor Rubin Battino has encountered during his extensive professional experience – from friends and support groups, from research and from practice – it is written to be thoroughly accessible and informative, inviting you to explore a wide range of techniques and methods that have proved to have a healing influence. These include:

- Guided imagery
- Nutrition
- Alternative medicine
- Meditation
- Support groups
- Structured writing
- Art therapy
- Acupuncture
- Relaxation methods, including Jackobson's Progressive Relaxation technique and Benson's Relaxation Response Method.

Featuring a variety of exercises and techniques, and assessing the uses and benefits of each, *Coping* is a complete guide to facing serious illness with hope and resourcefulness. Packed with invaluable advice on practical subjects such as communicating with medical personnel, and concluding with an extensive appendix of useful contacts, this book is simply an invaluable reference and companion for everyone dealing with life-challenging disease.

Paperback   **256 pages**   **ISBN 1899836683**

Guided Imagery And Other Approaches To Healing
Rubin Battino MS

This book explores in detail the most powerful methods of healing. While focusing on Guided Imagery, a healing technique that fully exploits the connection between mind and body, it also extends its analysis to other healing techniques, including psychotherapy-based methods and alternative therapies, encouraging a multi-modal approach to healing. An essentially practical and accessible healing manual, **Guided Imagery** presents a breakdown of published guided imagery scripts, while investigating the language used in guided imagery, the skills required in rapport-building, and the most effective methods in inducing a state of relaxation. Pioneering new bonding and fusion healing methods, **Guided Imagery** also incorporates a useful section on preparing patients for surgery, and a chapter on Nutrition and Healing, by nutrition expert A. Ira Fritz PhD, plus a chapter on Native American Healing Traditions, by Native American healer Helena Sheehan PhD. Designed as a resource for health professionals, **Guided Imagery**, meticulously researched and authoritative, is essential reading for doctors, nurses, psychologists, counsellors and all those involved or interested in healing.

"Well chosen, illuminating clinical examples abound, with eminently useful imagery suggestions for practitioner and patient."
– *Belleruth Naparstek, LISW, author of Staying Well with Guided Imagery.*

Hardback   **400 pages**   **ISBN** 1899836446

Also available:
2 audiotape set of guided imagery scripts – 113 mins.
ISBN 1899836594

Scripts and Strategies in Hypnotherapy
Roger P. Allen

The use of scripts in induction procedures provides an essential framework upon which to build successful therapy sessions. Written by a practising hypnotherapist, this is a rich, comprehensive source of scripts and strategies to be used by hypnotherapists of all levels of experience. Areas covered include inductions, deepeners and actual scripts for a wide range of problems, from nail biting to getting a good night's sleep, sports performance to past-life recall, pain management to resolving sexual problems. All scripts may be used as they stand or adapted for specific situations.

"*Scripts and Strategies in Hypnotherapy* **provides an imaginative source of scripts covering the most commonly met cases. For the newly qualified therapist, it is a useful addition and for the more experienced it is a source of inspiration.**" – *European Journal of Clinical Hypnosis.*

"**The most genuinely useful book on the subject to appear for years.**"– *Ormond McGill, 'Dean of American Hypnotists'.*

"**An essential addition to any hypnotherapist's library. I will use it again and again and again.**"– *Paul Dyer PhD.*

"**Imaginative, practical and, quite simply, essential for anyone getting started in hypnotherapy.**" – *Martin Roberts PhD, author of Change Management Excellence.*

Paperback   **176 pages**   **ISBN 1899836462**

Scripts and Strategies in Hypnotherapy Volume II
Roger P. Allen

The first volume of **Scripts And Strategies In Hypnotherapy** is now joined by **Scripts and Strategies in Hypnotherapy Volume II,** an indispensable collection of further scripts for hypnotherapists that may be used as they stand, or adapted for specific situations. Areas covered include inductions, deepeners and actual scripts, and strategies for a wide range of problems, from nail biting, smoking cessation and weight loss, to amnesia, anxiety and panic attacks.

Hardback   **256 pages**   **ISBN 1899836691**

Creative Intelligence:
Korzybski, Non-Aristotelian Thinking and Eastern Realization
Ted Falconar

Albert Einstein thought in an entirely different way from ordinary people, and the theorist Alfred Korzybski wanted to know why. Studying Einstein's unique thought processes in his extensive study *Science and Sanity*, he explained and explored this genius way of thinking, and named it Non-Aristotelian Thinking. Korzybski's Non-Aristotelian Thinking involves seeing events as they really are, and not as they are presented to us through the illusion of words and memory. It stresses how no one thing is like anything else – that even two pins are never the same; and that the word can never contain what it names.

Creative Intelligence extends Korzybski's concept by weaving into its fabric insights from Eastern philosophies of Realization (the seeing of reality) and Liberation (the aim of life). It teaches us, step-by-step, to 'unlearn' Aristotelian learning – that rigid pattern of thought that we are indoctrinated with from birth – and to escape the confines of memory, association and, most importantly, words.

"The ideas in this book can transform your life."
– *Dr David Shephard.*

Paperback   **160 pages**   **ISBN 1899836497**

Hypnotic Language:
Its Structure and Use
John Burton EdD & Bob G. Bodenhamer DMin

This remarkable book examines the structures of the hypnotic sentence, and the very cognitive dimensions that allow hypnotic language to be effective in changing our minds. Defining the three facets that allow the mind to be susceptible to hypnotic language patterns, **Hypnotic Language** puts these insights into practice in case examples that demonstrate the application and effect of hypnotic language. Teaching us how to create the most effective hypnotic scripts, it provides new language patterns that address beliefs, time orientation, perception, spiritual matters and states of mind, and devises new hypnotic language applications that emphasise the importance of Gestalt principles and cognitive factors.

An invaluable resource for hypnotherapists, psychologists, NLP practitioners and counsellors, **Hypnotic Language** promotes a new and deeper understanding of hypnotic language, clearly defining the divide between the conscious and unconscious mind – and those language paths that link the two. Providing a wealth of scripts for hypnotic trance, it presents innovative and original ways to induce cognitive change that enable you to access your unconscious mind – and the infinite resources it holds.

"Occasionally I pick up a book and find myself wishing that I had written it. Hypnotic Language is just such a book."
– Roger P. Allen, Dp Hyp PsyV

Hardback   **320 pages**   **ISBN 1899836357**

Hypnosis: A Comprehensive Guide
Tad James MS, PhD with Lorraine Flores & Jack Schober

Research shows that many people react differently to different kinds of hypnotic induction – yet many hypnotherapists are confined to using only one technique. This book makes three radically different and significant types of hypnosis easy to use in daily hypnosis work, examining in detail the techniques of Erickson, Estabrooks and Elman. Exploring methods that employ Direct Authoritarian and Indirect Permissive approaches, **Hypnosis** progresses beyond these approaches to describe the inductions pioneered by Dave Elman: a technique that places responsibility for hypnosis on the client. An invaluable resource for all trainers and therapists.

> **"This book is an excellent introductory text for students just beginning to study the art and science of hypnosis. For those already knowledgeable about hypnosis, there are many nuances that will enable you to increase the elegance of your work."**
> – *David Shephard PhD, Master Trainer of NLP, Director of Research and Training, The Performance Partnership, London, UK.*

Hardback   **240 pages**   **ISBN** 1899836454

Rapid Cognitive Therapy: The Professional Therapist's Guide To Rapid Change Work
Georges Philips & Terence Watts

As the title suggests, this book presents a brief psychotherapeutic approach to working with clients. What it doesn't tell you is that this book reaches way beyond a description of principles and outline of methods and techniques, to provide an easy-to-understand technology for all. Nearly all the techniques here can be used as adjuncts to conventional behaviourist and analytical approaches to therapy including NLP and Gestalt work. As well as describing the art of RCT, the authors have provided the therapist with the means to get started quickly by outlining the structures for the first few sessions as well as giving full scripts for analytical and non-analytical work with the client.

> **"Written by two excellent and experienced therapists, [Rapid Cognitive Therapy joins] the ranks of modern publications in the domain of psychotherapeutic approaches."**
> – *Professor V. M. Mathew, President, British Medical Hypnotherapy Examination Board.*

Hardback   **272 pages**   **ISBN** 1899836373

USA & Canada *orders to:*

LPC Group
1436 West Randolph Street, Chicago, Illinois, 60607
Tel: 800-626-4330, Fax: 800-334-3892
www.lpcgroup.com

Australasia *orders to:*

Footprint Books Pty Ltd
101 McCarrs Creek Road, PO Box 418, Church Point
Sydney NSW 2105, Australia
Tel: +61 2 9997 3973, Fax: +61 2 9997 3185
E-mail: footprintbooks@ozemail.com.au

UK & Rest of World *orders to:*

The Anglo American Book Company Ltd.
Crown Buildings, Bancyfelin, Carmarthen, Wales SA33 5ND
Tel: +44 (0)1267 211880/211886, Fax: +44 (0)1267 211882
E-mail: books@anglo-american.co.uk
www.anglo-american.co.uk